THE **Denuclearization**

OF LATIN AMERICA

by ALFONSO GARCÍA ROBLES

TRANSLATED BY MARJORIE URQUIDI

Carnegie Endowment for International Peace ▪ 1967

. . . estamos convencidos de que, o el mundo acaba con las armas nucleares, o las armas nucleares acaban con el mundo.

GUSTAVO DÍAZ ORDAZ

President of the United Mexican States ·

Table of Contents

Part Two INTERNATIONAL DOCUMENTS

Preface

Ever since the end of the Second World War, the international community has been deeply concerned with what the United Nations Charter in one place refers to as "disarmament and the regulation of armaments" and in another as "the regulation of armaments, and possible disarmament." The initial goal of international efforts—and the primary goal throughout this period—was to ensure that nuclear energy would be used to promote the welfare of human kind and not lead to its destruction. The first resolution of the General Assembly of the United Nations, adopted at its first session in London in January 1946, called for the control of atomic energy to the extent necessary to ensure its use only for peaceful purposes, and the elimination of nuclear weapons from national armaments under a system of effective safeguards.

Over the years a tremendous amount of thought and energy has been invested in the attempt to grapple with the baffling issues posed by the discovery of nuclear energy and the invention of nuclear weapons. The problems have been discussed at every session of the General Assembly. At one time or another they have been raised at every level of practically every branch of national governments, and they have become of increasing interest to the intellectual community in universities and other institutions. Thus far there has been very little success.

Two main avenues have been explored. First, there are the various comprehensive plans, such as the so-called "Baruch Plan" in the 1940s for establishing an international authority to own, manage, and control all atomic energy activities throughout the world; the plans for comprehensive balanced reduction of armaments and prohibition of nuclear weapons during the 1950s; and plans for general and complete disarmament during the 1960s. Second, there have been parallel efforts during this entire period to achieve less ambitious measures of disarmament or of arms regulation and control. This second approach has sometimes been called the step-by-step method, the achievement of partial measures of disarmament, measures for arms control, confidence-building measures, arms limitation measures, and, more recently, simply "collateral measures" that could facilitate the ultimate achievement of general and complete disarmament.

Despite the unremitting efforts over the last two decades, no agreements have been reached on general disarmament and only very limited agreements on collateral measures. In the latter field, 1963 stands out as a banner year. In June of that year, what is known as the "hot line" communications link was established between Moscow and Washington as an arms control or confidence-building measure which could help to avert war by miscalculation, accident, or breakdown in communications; in August, the partial test ban treaty prohibiting nuclear weapon tests in the atmosphere, outer space, and underwater was signed in Moscow (and subsequently signed or acceded to by more than 100 states); and in October the General Assembly of the United Nations called for a permanent ban on nuclear and mass destruction weapons in outer space, and welcomed the expressions of intention by the Soviet Union and the United States to that effect.

During the past decade most of the disarmament efforts have been directed toward achieving two goals which, though not strictly speaking actual "disarmament," were important collateral measures: one, to halt all nuclear weapon tests including underground ones, and two, to prevent the proliferation of nuclear weapons. The search for both goals proceeded at first on a global and comprehensive basis. As it became increasingly clear that these efforts were not to be crowned with early success, more modest approaches were sought on a partial or regional basis.

In 1958, the so-called "Rapacki Plan" was proposed by the Foreign Minister of Poland for the denuclearization of Central Europe, that is, Poland, Czechoslovakia, and East and West Germany. Since that time various proposals have been put forward for the denuclearization of other areas of the world including the Balkans, the Middle East, the Mediterranean, Northern Europe, the Far East, and, more recently, Latin America and Africa. All of these plans, except those concerning Latin America and Africa, failed to make progress because of the complex political and strategic factors involved. In general, these denuclearization proposals were supported by the Eastern or Communist states; but the proposals affecting Europe and Asia were opposed by the Western powers who considered them to be "unbalanced" in the sense that they would involve the withdrawal of Western nuclear bases and would thus give some military and political advantages to the Eastern or Communist states at the expense of the West. It was argued by the Western powers that any plans for denuclearized or nuclear-free zones would have to be such as not to upset the existing military balance, that they should come about as a result of the initiative of the main countries in the area, and that they should be subject to verification to prevent the possibility of clandestine evasion.

The Cuban crisis of October 1962 suddenly and dramatically confronted the states of Latin America with the fact that their area of the world had become involved in the strategic plans and rivalries of the nuclear powers. Men of vision in the area turned their thoughts to ways of avoiding any possibility of a recurrence of the Cuban experience in some other country of Latin America. They also wished to preclude even the relatively remote possibility of a nuclear arms race among the countries of their area.

Five Latin American presidents, those of Bolivia, Brazil, Chile, Ecuador, and Mexico expressed their views on this in their Joint Declaration of 29 April 1963 on the denuclearization of Latin America, and in November of that year the General Assembly of the United Nations adopted a resolution approving the idea. On the initiative of the government of Mexico, a Preparatory Commission for the Denuclearization of Latin America was established in November 1964 at a Preliminary Meeting held in Mexico City.

With the assistance of a permanent secretariat provided by Mexico at the Commission's request, and with the support of the Secretary-General of the United Nations and technical assistance furnished by him, the Preparatory Commission has made definite progress toward achieving a treaty for a nuclear-free zone in Latin America. Indeed, more progress has been made toward the elaboration of a treaty for the denuclearization of Latin America than in the case of any other area of the world, and valuable new ground has been broken. There are encouraging prospects that a treaty for at least a part of the area, if not the whole, will be signed during the course of the forthcoming year.

The Preparatory Commission now, after three sessions, has worked out the draft of a treaty for the denuclearization of Latin America which provides that the territories of the countries that become parties to the treaty will be free of all testing, production, stationing, deployment, or use of nuclear weapons. The draft contains provisions for verification to ensure that all the signatories will abide by the terms of the treaty, and creates permanent organs to supervise the operation of the treaty. Although there is as yet no agreement on the requirements for the entry into force of the treaty, most of the provisions of the draft treaty have been agreed to.

It would be misleading, however, to assume that all the major issues have been solved. A number of tough and complex questions of great importance still remain. Is it necessary that all states of Latin America and, in particular, Cuba, should become parties to the treaty before its entry into force, or would a treaty limited to only part of the zone be acceptable and effective? Would it be necessary for all countries having "international responsibility for territories" situated in the Caribbean, or in Latin America (France, the Netherlands, the United Kingdom, and the United States) to agree that their territories should be included, or would the treaty be workable without the inclusion of all these dependent territories? Would it be necessary for all five of the nuclear powers—the United States, the Soviet Union, the United Kingdom, France, and the People's Republic of China—to undertake to respect the zone, or would it be sufficient if they were bound by the ordinary rules of international law and of the United Nations Charter to respect the sovereign independence and territory of the countries which become part of the nuclear-free zone?

A number of thoughtful leaders in the area appear to believe that, although the prospects of a nuclear arms race developing in Latin America are somewhat further removed than in some other areas of the world, it would, nevertheless, be wise to take measures to prevent such an arms race precisely because at the present time it is easier to do so. They seem to understand, too, that if even one or two countries within the area developed or acquired nuclear weapons, the spread would not stop there but could eventually include a half-dozen or more countries.

Another factor which seems to motivate Latin American statesmen is that the enormous costs involved in building a few atom bombs, together with the endless and increasing expense of developing more sophisticated weapons and delivery systems, would prevent their dealing adequately with the pressing economic and social problems of the area. Understandably, they wish to avoid a ruinous and senseless nuclear arms race that would embroil them in the nuclear strategic plans and policies of the nuclear powers. At the same time they are interested in obtaining the benefits of the peaceful uses and application of atomic energy and insist that any denuclearization treaty should present no bar of any kind to the full development and exploitation of these peaceful uses.

The only previous instances of denuclearization are Antarctica, which was demilitarized as well as denuclearized by the Antarctica Treaty of 1959, and outer space, which was dealt with in the General Assembly resolution in October 1963, and is now the subject of final negotiations for a treaty to exclude nuclear weapons from outer space. Agreement on denuclearization in these two cases was, of course, facilitated by the fact that there were no inhabitants and very few, if any, vested military or economic interests in them. While the same considerations do not apply to Latin America, nevertheless a number of factors peculiar to Latin America make it, on the whole, more susceptible than other areas of the globe to denuclearization. There are no "opposing sides," so to speak, no balance of power problems, no confrontation of East-West power blocs, and no nuclear weapons or bases within the area. Moreover, most of the countries have much in common including culture, tradition, and heritage. Consequently, this area, perhaps more than any other inhabited area of the world, has a better opportunity to pioneer in the creation of the first real denuclearized zone.

The successful denuclearization of Latin America, whether in whole or in part, would have great importance not only to the countries who participate and to their region but also to the entire world. The Latin American treaty could, for example, particularly if it worked well in practice, become a model for similar treaties in Africa and perhaps for other areas of the world. It would reduce the size of the global nonproliferation problem by removing the countries of the treaty zone from the list of potential military nuclear powers. It should also give impetus to other measures of disarmament and help to stimulate the efforts of the Eighteen-Nation Disarmament Committee in Geneva.

As United Nations Secretary-General Thant has stated, "Success in their endeavours will not only be an achievement of great benefit to the States of Latin America, militarily, politically, economically and socially; it can indeed be of great importance to the world at large. It may well have a catalytic effect on other initiatives for denuclearization, for preventing the further spread of nuclear weapons and for other measures of disarmament."

The fourth session of the Preparatory Commission for the Denuclearization of Latin America will be convening in Mexico on 31 January 1967. This session may be of crucial importance to the success or failure of what has been the most encouraging effort to date to achieve a nuclear-free zone. At this time it does not seem likely that all the countries of the area, despite their active sympathy with the idea, or all the governments administering territories within the zone, or all five of the present nuclear powers, will give their full support to a treaty for the denuclearization of Latin America. Nevertheless, if enough of them do so, and an agreed treaty emerges, even if only for part of the area, the nations of Latin America, as a result of their own initiative and peaceful desires and intentions, will have erected an important milestone along the long and difficult road toward disarmament. They will have contributed in a concrete way to the promotion of international peace and security.

The efforts of the Latin American states to achieve a nuclear-free zone in their part of the world have received less public notice than they deserve. Moreover the documentary record is little known and difficult to come by. It is the hope of the Carnegie Endowment that the publication of this little book will help to overcome both of these shortcomings.

The author, Dr. Alfonso García Robles, has been closely associated with the work of the United Nations since its inception, and has been particularly concerned with disarmament matters. As a member of the Mexican Delegation to the San Francisco Conference on International Organization in 1945, he participated in the drafting of the United Nations Charter. From 1946 to 1957, he was the Director of the Political Affairs Division of the United Nations Secretariat and, as such, was actively engaged in a number of important assignments. In 1957 he returned to the Mexican Foreign Service. Now Under-Secretary for Foreign Affairs, he has held several ambassadorial posts. He has represented his government at nearly all sessions of the United Nations General Assembly since 1957 and in recent years has been Chairman of the Mexican Delegation. He has lectured at a number of universities in Mexico, Europe, and the United States, and has written several books on international and legal questions. Dr. García Robles has played a leading role in the matter of the denuclearization of Latin America from the time it was first raised by the five presidents in April 1963, as well as in the presentation and the adoption of Resolution 1911 (XVIII) by the General Assembly in November 1963. Since his election as Chairman of the Preliminary Meeting and of the Preparatory Commission for the Denuclearization of Latin America in 1964, he has been the main moving spirit in promoting the concept. There is no person better qualified to write on the subject.

November 1966

Joseph E. Johnson
President, Carnegie Endowment
for International Peace

Introduction

This may be the first book published in English on the denuclearization of Latin America—an enterprise which in less than two years has
captured the interest and enthusiastic support of all the countries in
that region.

The primary purpose of this volume is to furnish objective information for a thorough understanding and evaluation of the work begun
by the Latin American countries in November 1964. It contains the
principal speeches delivered at international meetings by the author,
who has been closely concerned with the project since its initiation
and has participated directly in almost all the work related to it, and
the most important official documents on the subject.

The texts will give the reader a clear and precise idea of the origin,
scope, and objectives of the activities in which Latin America has been
pioneering with zeal and perseverance. The events leading toward the
conclusion of a universally respected treaty to ensure the denuclearization of the region may be divided into seven stages:

1. The Joint Declaration of 29 April 1963, in which the heads of state
   of five Latin American republics announced that their respective
   governments were willing to sign a Latin American multilateral
   agreement under which the countries would undertake not "to
   manufacture, store, or test nuclear weapons or devices for launching
   nuclear weapons."

2. United Nations General Assembly Resolution 1911 (XVIII) of 27
   November 1963, in which the international community expressed
   its wholehearted support and encouragement of the declaration. It
   noted "with satisfaction" the initiative and expressed the hope that
   the Latin American states would initiate studies "concerning the

measures that should be agreed upon with a view to achieving the aims of the said declaration."

3. The Preliminary Session on the Denuclearization of Latin America was held in Mexico City from 23 to 27 November 1964. Acting as a constituent assembly, it established a Preparatory Commission for Denuclearization of Latin America, with headquarters in Mexico City, consisting of the seventeen participating Latin American republics and those countries which might subsequently adhere to the resolution. It specifically instructed the Preparatory Commission "to prepare a preliminary draft of a multilateral treaty for the denuclearization of Latin America and, to this end, to conduct any prior studies and take any prior steps that it deems necessary," and recommended procedures to be followed for this task.

4. The First Session of the Preparatory Commission took place in Mexico City from 15 to 22 March 1965. Eighteen Latin American republics attended, as well as observers from Guatemala, the Netherlands, and Yugoslavia. This meeting set up a Coordinating Committee and three Working Groups, of which two were to carry out their activities at United Nations Headquarters in New York City and one in Mexico City, and defined a number of urgent tasks. It also fixed 23 August 1965 as the date and Mexico City as the place of the Second Session of the Preparatory Commission.

5. The Second Session of the Preparatory Commission was held in Mexico City from 23 August to 2 September 1965 with the participation of nineteen Latin American republics and the presence of observers from the United States of America, Canada, and eight extra-continental states. On this occasion the Commission took several important decisions: (a) to transmit to the governments of the member states a preliminary draft of articles on verification, inspection, and control prepared by Working Group B, requesting each government to send its comments to the Secretariat of the Commission not later than 15 January 1966; (b) to approve a complete declaration of principles to serve as a basis for the Preamble to the Preliminary Draft of the Treaty for the Denuclearization of Latin America drawn up by the Commission; (c) to establish a Negotiating Committee consisting of the Chairman of the Commission and the Chairman of Working Groups A and C, who during the twentieth session of the General Assembly of the United Nations would make every effort to speed up the work assigned to those Groups; and (d) to urge the governments of the member states to concentrate their efforts and take all the measures they deem necessary to assist the Commission in drawing up the Preliminary Draft Treaty at its third session.

6. The Coordinating Committee met in February and March 1966. In accordance with Resolution 9 (II) of the Commission and in performance of the general functions assigned to it by the Commission in Resolution 1 (I), the Committee prepared a working paper in the form of a Preliminary Draft Treaty covering all the questions which the Commission would have to resolve in order to draw up the final Treaty for the Denuclearization of Latin America.

7. The Third Session of the Preparatory Commission for Denuclearization of Latin America took place in Mexico City from 19 April to 4 May 1966. Unanimous approval was accorded a basic document entitled "Proposals for the Preparation of the Treaty for the Denuclearization of Latin America," which will have as prominent a place in the history of the future Treaty as that of the Dumbarton Oaks Proposals in the history of the United Nations. The Proposals were transmitted to member governments with the request that they make known "any observations they see fit to make" and at the same time that "such observations be drafted preferably in the form of specific amendments to the articles of the document."

In its Resolution 14 (III) approving the Proposals, the Commission also asked its Chairman to transmit them to several non-member states, including the nuclear powers, and to request that they inform him of the attitude they anticipate taking toward such a treaty. The Governments of three of the nuclear powers—France, Great Britain, and the United States of America—have already replied to the respective notes of the President.

In its Resolution 12 (III), the Commission instructed the Negotiating Committee to make informal inquiries to ascertain "whether the Government of the People's Republic of China would be prepared to undertake to respect the legal instrument for the denuclearization of Latin America." On 29 August 1966 the Committee presented a report on the results of its activities.

The Commission now consists of twenty-one members, with Jamaica and Trinidad and Tobago added to the nineteen Latin American republics, and it is attended by observers from eighteen countries extending over four continents. Although the Fourth Session of the Preparatory Commission was convoked for 30 August 1966, several of the members requested that it be postponed in order to have more time for informal consultations that would contribute to the "creation of the most favorable conditions for the preparation of the Draft of the the Treaty for the Denuclearization of Latin America." The Commission, therefore, agreed in its Resolution 19 (IV) to postpone its next meeting until 31 January 1967.

General agreement has been reached on about 90 per cent of the

Treaty's contents, and no insuperable difficulties stand in the way of agreement on the remaining 10 per cent. In view of the progress already achieved, the Commission may be expected to complete its task successfully at its next session, thereby fulfilling the hopes of the people of Latin America and serving as a catalyst to world action.

In any discussion of the denuclearization of Latin America, it should be recalled that the term "denuclearization," within the context of the relevant declarations and resolutions, refers exclusively to military denuclearization. The Preliminary Session on the Denuclearization of Latin America was careful to make clear in its first resolution that, for the purposes of the Latin American countries, denuclearization means "the absence of nuclear weapons and nuclear launching devices." Bearing in mind the importance of nuclear energy for economic and scientific development, it stressed "the advisability of promoting international cooperation for the peaceful use of nuclear energy, especially for the benefit of the developing countries."

Under the terms of the Treaty, the peaceful use of atomic energy is not only permitted but encouraged, whereas nuclear weapons are absolutely and totally prohibited—irrespective of the state controlling them—within the geographical area to which the Treaty would apply. The possibility that this prohibition may be universally recognized as legally binding has implications of transcendental significance.

The ban on nuclear tests in the atmosphere, concluded in August 1963 under the Moscow Treaty, has made us begin to forget the repeated warnings of thousands of scientists about the myriad and terrible effects of a nuclear explosion. It is therefore useful to review some basic facts concerning the consequences of a nuclear conflagration, catastrophic for all mankind but to a much greater degree for the people living in the territories where nuclear weapons and launching devices exist.

Eminent scientists have calculated—and their calculations are substantially in agreement with those recently published by the Secretary of Defense of one of the two leading nuclear powers—the effects of a nuclear war, which can be summarized as follows:

1. About 75 per cent of the population of the country under attack— and the same proportion of the population of the aggressor country, as the result of immediate reprisals—would either be killed instantaneously by the terrible explosive and thermal effects of the bombs or would perish during the next two months from radiation received in the first twenty-four hours after the bombing.
2. A substantial part of the remaining 25 per cent would also die gradually as a consequence of radioactivity, of which an estimated 80 per cent would fall on the bombed territories.

3. The other 20 per cent of the fallout would spread more or less evenly over the world's surface. Mankind would be seriously threatened, not so much because of direct exposure to the radio-activity generated by the explosions, but indirectly through a chain reaction ending in the presence of substances in the food that can cause irreparable damage to the body, especially to the genes. It has been estimated that between 100 million and 300 million infants would be born dead or with deformities often bordering on the monstrous as the result of a war employing a nuclear explosion of 50,000 megatons (a megaton is equal in yield to a million tons of TNT, which was the most destructive explosive known prior to the nuclear era).

The dangers are of such magnitude that distinguished scientists of several nationalities have predicted that a large-scale nuclear war might change man's plasma in such a way that the human species, as we know it, could not survive and that the whole earth might eventually become uninhabitable.

The foregoing explains why those living in Latin America, which is fortunately free of nuclear weapons, can rightly consider that their duty is to strive to make this situation a permanent and immutable one through a multilateral treaty that will be universally respected.

Furthermore, a treaty for the denuclearization of Latin America not only would spare this region the slaughter that a nuclear conflagration would inevitably inflict on countries possessing nuclear weapons, but would also constitute—and herein lies one of its principal merits—an important contribution to the coordinated program of disarmament envisaged in 1954 by the General Assembly of the United Nations in its Resolution 808 (IX) which included "the total prohibition of the use and manufacture of nuclear weapons and weapons of mass destruction of every type, together with the conversion of existing stocks of nuclear weapons for peaceful purposes."

When it enters into force, the Treaty for the Denuclearization of Latin America will be the first step, always the most difficult, toward realizing the fervently desired goal of people all over the world. If, as may logically be expected, other regional treaties for denuclearization should be concluded, great progress will have been made along the path leading to universal denuclearization.

Latin America, faithful to its tradition of international cooperation, will have labored once more not only on behalf of its own peoples, but also for the good of mankind.

ALFONSO GARCÍA ROBLES
Chairman of the Preparatory Commission for the Denuclearization of Latin America
United Nations, New York, October 1966.

Part One SPEECHES IN INTERNATIONAL FORUMS

1 Speech Delivered at the 1333rd Meeting of the First Committee of the General Assembly of the United Nations ▪ on 11 November 1963

As a result of the reflection which must—or should—precede any of our statements in the debates of the United Nations, I have decided to limit this statement to a kind of trilogy in which I shall examine the following points:

I shall deal, first, with the Joint Declaration of 29 April 1963,[1] referred to in the penultimate preambular paragraph and the first operative paragraph of the joint draft resolution,[2] which was submitted to our Committee as document A/C.1/L.329 by ten Latin American states, including Mexico; second, with the contents and scope of the draft resolution itself; and, finally, with some of the main aspects of those parts of the debate on the second item of the agenda of the First Committee where direct or indirect allusion was made to the third item on the agenda, which only today we have begun to discuss formally.

I shall begin by summarizing the origin, scope, and objectives of the declaration on the denuclearization of Latin America. Such a procedure is not only appropriate but indispensable, inasmuch as the

[1] The text of the Declaration appears below as Section 12.

[2] The co-sponsors of the joint draft resolution were, in addition to Mexico: Bolivia, Brazil, Costa Rica, Chile, Ecuador, El Salvador, Haiti, Panama, and Uruguay. The text of the joint draft resolution is identical with the resolution approved by the General Assembly which is reproduced below as Section 13.

3

prominence given this declaration in the joint draft resolution requires, in our opinion, that the main background as well as the text and ideals of the declaration go into the records of the First Committee—just as they went into the verbatim record of the 128th meeting of the Conference of the Eighteen-Nation Disarmament Commission held in Geneva on 6 May 1963.

My country is very honored that the initiative of this declaration came from the President of Mexico, Adolfo López Mateos, who, on 21 March 1963, addressed letters[3] to the presidents of Bolivia, Brazil, Chile, and Ecuador concerning "a subject that is linked to the welfare of this region of the world in which we live," namely, the denuclearization of Latin America.

As a preamble or introduction, the head of the Mexican government referred to three earlier declarations which help to place his initiative in its proper context. He first recalled Mexico's initial address to the Eighteen-Nation Disarmament Committee by Manuel Tello, Minister of Foreign Affairs who, following presidential instructions, made this statement:

In our view, pending worldwide agreement, denuclearization could, can, and should be brought about through voluntary and free decisions by States. Thus, the Mexican Government has resolved neither to possess nor to admit to its national territory nuclear weapons of any sort or any vehicles that might be used for their delivery. While we, of course, lack the technical or economic resources to take such action, our attitude would be the same even if that were not the case. Similarly, we supported both by our statements and by our votes the resolutions submitted with a view to preventing the spread of nuclear weapons.[4]

Explaining the reason for the instructions given for the preparation of the above speech, President López Mateos said in his letter to the four Latin American presidents that he was firmly convinced that "we are living at a dramatic moment, a moment that demands from each and every one of us—but especially from those of us who have received the mandate to interpret the will of our peoples—a resolute and consistent conduct aimed at the preservation of life itself."

The President of Mexico went on in his letter to refer to the second declaration that led up to his initiative. This was the draft resolution presented by the delegation of Brazil and supported by the delegations of Bolivia, Chile, and Ecuador at the seventeenth regular session of the General Assembly of the United Nations. He took note with "special pleasure" of a document which was intended "to fulfill an ideal cher-

[3] See *Presencia Internacional de Adolfo López Mateos* (Mexico City: Talleres Gráficos de la Nación, 1963), pp. 621–624.
[4] United Nations Doc. ENDC/PV.7, 22 Mar. 1962.

ished by all Latin Americans, the denuclearization of our region."

The third and last declaration mentioned in the letter of the President of Mexico was that which he had solemnly made in December 1962 to the effect that his government was prepared "to sign a commitment if a substantial number or all of the Latin American Republics would also undertake, either by unilateral or by a specific multilateral agreement, not to acquire by any right or to permit for any reason on their national territory the stockpiling or transporting of nuclear weapons or the installation of launching sites for such weapons."

Having presented this background, President López Mateos explained his ideas to the four other presidents as follows:

Thus, Mr. President, I come to the problem that now confronts Latin American leaders: the choice of suitable means for achieving the aspiration which, in the light of what I have said, I do not hesitate to describe as one that we share.

After deep reflection, I have decided that the attention of the illustrious Heads of States co-sponsoring the above-mentioned draft resolution should be drawn to the necessity of bending every effort to adopt measures to promote the denuclearization of Latin America. I was led to this conclusion by the conviction that it is up to these four countries, together with my own, to take again the initiative.

In addressing you, Mr. President, I am addressing a statesman who has given much proof of political maturity in guiding his people. I am sure that the experience that has made you so outstanding will be particularly helpful in the task we have before us.

One method which I believe might be successful would be for the Presidents of Brazil, Chile, Ecuador, and Mexico to make public a joint declaration wherein we would announce our readiness to sign a multilateral agreement with the other countries of Latin America, setting forth our commitment not to manufacture, receive, store, or test nuclear weapons or devices for launching such weapons. This declaration would express the hope that the other Latin American countries might accede to it, so that it would eventually become a kind of charter liberating our peoples from all nuclear threat. I do not believe that I am guilty of over-optimism when I say that such a document would also have a very beneficial effect on the efforts that are now being carried out both in the General Assembly of the United Nations and in the Disarmament Committee to banish forever the specter of nuclear war.

The suggestion of the President of Mexico was honored by an immediate and enthusiastic response on the part of the leaders of the four countries to whom it had been addressed.[5]

In his reply, dated 8 April 1963, the President of Brazil described

[5] The complete text of the letters of the four presidents is published in the monthly journal of the Ministry of Foreign Affairs of Mexico, *México de Hoy*, No. 151 (May 1963), pp. 84–86.

the initiative of his Mexican colleague as "a vital contribution to the improvement of international relations," and he called it a "felicitous and transcendental initiative taken by that great and noble country in the interests of international peace and security." The President of Chile, in his reply of 16 April, stated that he agreed entirely with the text of the proposed declaration. He expressed his conviction that if it was successful in achieving its objectives, it would have helped "the peace efforts of the Eighteen-Nation Committee;" he went on to say that "an important step would have been taken toward general and complete disarmament," and that it would have "faithfully interpreted the desire for peace on this continent." The President of Bolivia, in his letter of 18 April, wholeheartedly agreed with the points of view expressed by the President of Mexico and described the proposed declaration as a "valuable precedent in the task of consolidating the peace-loving tradition of the peoples of the hemisphere." Finally, in a letter dated 22 April, the President of Ecuador gave his support to the Mexican initiative, which he called "most valuable," and he expressed the opinion that the proposed declaration would constitute "a transcendental and definitive step which, if followed by the other peoples of America, would permit us to gaze into the future with greater tranquility and confidence."

As soon as the President of Mexico had received the encouraging replies of the other four Latin American presidents, he addressed a message[6] to the Mexican people by radio and television on 29 April 1963. After paying "warm tribute" to the Presidents of Bolivia, Brazil, Chile, and Ecuador, he announced that by common agreement the declaration on the denuclearization of Latin America was from that moment solemnly adopted by the five Latin American states. Analogous statements were made simultaneously in the capitals of the other four countries concerned.

In this same message, President López Mateos wanted to remove all possibility of a misinterpretation of the reasons which had led him to address, first of all, only four of the heads of state of Latin American countries. He stated:

I now have only to explain to you why, although Mexico has always been known for its feelings of fraternal friendship and respect toward each and every one of the Latin American peoples, I decided, in this first phase of our enterprise, to address only the Heads of State that I have mentioned. The reason is simply that these four countries had the honor of co-sponsoring, at the last session of the General Assembly of the United Nations, a draft resolution which proposed the denuclearization of Latin America. At the request of the co-sponsors of the draft, discussion of this document was

[6] See *Presencia Internacional . . .*, op. cit., pp. 624–627.

postponed. I therefore believed that I should suggest to these four States that it would be desirable to invite the other sister Republics to join us in our efforts to proscribe nuclear threats from Latin American lands. Furthermore, I am happy to announce that I shall lose no time in addressing fraternal messages to the Heads of State of the other Latin American countries, expressing the most fervent hope that we shall be able to count on their invaluable collaboration in this common enterprise.

In this same message, parts of which I am quoting, the President of Mexico synthesized the objectives sought in his initiative and the principles underlying it.

In the present circumstances of a "cold war" where the great Power groups at every moment confront one another from their respective positions of force, our country's role is to be a moderating influence. The devotion of the Mexican people to peace, furthermore, demanded that Mexico join its efforts with those of other States similarly disposed. By their example, they would encourage the great Powers to persist in their search for formulas leading to general and complete disarmament. . . .

For various reasons which are common knowledge the Eighteen-Nation Committee has so far been prevented from achieving its noble objective, general and complete disarmament. Obviously, pending worldwide agreement, an attempt should be made to denuclearize large geographical zones by the sovereign decision of the States composing them.

Latin America, which has so distinguished itself for its valuable contribution to the development of the great principles of law and justice, is in an ideal position to become one of these regions.

It was on this same solemn occasion that the Mexican people were first informed of the text of the Joint Declaration on the Denuclearization of Latin America.

I now come to the second part of this statement which, as I said earlier, will review the provisions of the joint draft resolution A/C.1/L.329. No explanation is needed for the first paragraph of the preamble, which obviously is inspired by and partly reproduces the first paragraph of the United Nations Charter.

The second paragraph of the preamble faithfully reflects in both form and content the respective preambles of the three General Assembly resolutions mentioned therein, which were approved without a single negative vote in the case of the first two and unanimously in the case of the third.

The text of the third paragraph of the preamble is a combination of the first two preambular paragraphs of United Nations General Assembly Resolution 1664 (XIV), which are incontrovertible; when this question was discussed two years ago, there was not a single representative, either in the debates of the First Committee or in those of the General Assembly, who raised any objection to these preambular paragraphs.

Nor does the first part of the fourth paragraph of the preamble require a lengthy explanation. I am sure that all the members of this Committee will agree that a self-evident truth is expressed in its statement that the Moscow Treaty signed on 5 August 1963 created a favorable atmosphere for the conclusion of other agreements on disarmament. Any doubts about this may be dispelled by glancing through the records of this Committee's meetings at the current eighteenth session where it will probably be seen that every speaker has made the same observation.

The connection referred to in the last part of the same paragraph, in addition to being obvious, is based on the texts of the resolutions cited therein; namely, 1649 (XIV) of 8 November 1961 and 1762 of 6 November 1962.

For the moment I shall omit the penultimate paragraph of the preamble, which refers to the Joint Declaration of the five Latin American presidents, in order to discuss it together with the first operative paragraph, to which it is closely linked.

The final paragraph of the preamble is self-explanatory at least to anyone who, on the one hand, is aware of Latin America's privileged position where no nuclear weapons exist and, on the other, reflects on the incalculable dangers to peace and the squandering of astronomical sums which would inevitably result from involvement of the Latin American countries in a nuclear arms race.

The penultimate paragraph of the preamble reproduces the words of the key paragraph of the Declaration on the Denuclearization of Latin America, to which I have referred at length in the first part of my statement. Although it still does not represent a legal commitment but only the solemn expression that the parties to it are willing to contract such a commitment, it is useful as a point of departure for the joint draft resolution, because it is the only international instrument of a multilateral character existing today on the denuclearization of Latin America.

The first operative paragraph will, I hope, be fully justified by my brief exposition of the following concrete facts.

Five days after the Joint Declaration of 29 April 1963 was made public, the Secretary-General of our Organization held a press conference at the Palais des Nations in Geneva. Questioned by a newspaper correspondent on this Declaration, he replied:

The mood of the United Nations General Assembly has always been in favor of the establishment of denuclearized zones in parts of the world. I think it was the feeling of most African nations last year and the year before that Africa should be made a denuclearized zone; and last week—actually a few days before I left New York—I received a communication from five Latin American Governments declaring their intention to make Latin America a denuclearized zone.

My personal feeling is that that attitude on the part of a growing number of Member States of the United Nations should be welcomed, because I feel very strongly that any denuclearized area would represent some kind of territorial disarmament. I interpret this trend as some kind of territorial disarmament—a trend which should be welcomed.[7]

On 6 May, three days after this press conference, the 128th meeting of the Eighteen-Nation Committee on Disarmament took place in Geneva. At that meeting, the representative of Brazil, Josué de Castro, and the representative of Mexico, Dr. Luis Padilla Nervo, officially presented to the Committee the Joint Declaration of the five presidents, giving a detailed exposition of its origin, objectives, and significance within the framework of disarmament.

Immediately after these statements, almost all the other members of the Committee expressed their opinion on the Declaration. Although the complete texts can easily be consulted in the record of the 128th meeting, I shall quote in illustration some of the more significant paragraphs, following the order in which they were made.

The representative of Nigeria stated:

The joint declaration of the five Latin American Presidents to turn Latin America into a denuclearized zone is indeed a commendable effort which my delegation fully endorses.[8]

The representative of Burma said:

The proliferation of nuclear weapons confronts mankind with the gravest of dangers. If the world is to succeed in its imperative task of eliminating all such weapons through general and complete disarmament, we must begin by taking all possible steps to prevent the problem from growing in magnitude and complexity through the further spread of nuclear weapons. We therefore welcome the present initiative of the five Latin American Presidents, and wish it all success in achieving its noble and worthy objective.

The representative of Italy declared:

My delegation fully understands and shares the noble aspirations behind that proposal. . . . In the case of the establishment of a denuclearized zone in Latin America, I think the requisite conditions are met, since the necessary military equilibrium is not affected.

That is the reason why the Italian delegation is convinced of the usefulness of the proposal made by the five Presidents. I would even say that my delega-

7 U.N. Press Services, Note to Correspondents, No. 2765.
8 This quotation and those that follow are reproduced in United Nations Doc. ENDC/PV.128.

9

spirit of the co-sponsors of the draft resolution who, when principles were not at stake, were ready to welcome the suggestions made to them by various delegations of the continent.

The only sentence in this paragraph to which some words might be added is the one recommending that studies be initiated "in the light of the principles of the Charter of the United Nations and of regional agreements." I would like to comment on this because some representatives of member states of other continents may not be familiar with inter-American organization. The "regional agreements" referred to are the Charter of the Organization of American States, also known as the Charter of Bogotá, and the Inter-American Treaty of Reciprocal Assistance, also known as the Treaty of Río de Janeiro.

For the benefit of the same representatives I shall add that the principles of these regional agreements are similar to those of the United Nations. Furthermore, in case of the slightest conflict between the regional instrument and the Charter of San Francisco, of course the latter would prevail by virtue of the provisions of Article 103, which stipulates: "In the event of a conflict between the obligations of the Members of the United Nations under the present Charter and their obligations under any other agreement, their obligations under the present Charter shall prevail."

The Charter of Bogotá, in one of its main articles, Article 102, which appears separately as Chapter XVI entitled "The United Nations," states even more clearly: "None of the provisions of this Charter shall be construed as impairing the rights and obligations of the Member States under the Charter of the United Nations."

Article 10 of the Treaty of Río de Janeiro says in almost identical words: "None of the provisions of this Treaty shall be construed as impairing the rights and obligations of the High Contracting Parties under the Charter of the United Nations."

Going on to operative paragraph 3 of the joint draft resolution, it should be noted that, in the light of Resolution 1665 (XVI) approved unanimously—I repeat, unanimously—on 4 December 1961, there would appear to be good reason to believe that the cooperation referred to in the paragraph may become a reality in due course, as the text of the paragraph trusts it will. It should not be forgotten that in the above-mentioned resolution the General Assembly called upon "all States" to cooperate in achieving the end set forth in the resolution in the following terms:

Calls upon all States, and in particular upon the States at present possessing nuclear weapons, to use their best endeavours to secure the conclusion of an international agreement containing provisions under which the nuclear States would refrain from relinquishing control of nuclear weapons and from transmitting the information necessary for their manufacture to States not possessing such weapons, and provisions under which States not possessing nuclear weapons would undertake not to manufacture or otherwise acquire control of such weapons.

Further on in the third part of my statement, when I deal with some declarations on denuclearized zones, which were made during the debate on the above topic, I shall make known my delegation's attitude on a matter of juridical principle which is related to the aspects discussed both in paragraph 2 and 3 of the joint draft resolution.

The final paragraph, number 4, of the draft resolution surely needs no comment. All of us who have participated in the meetings of the organs of the United Nations are well aware of the effective and fruitful work—all the more so because it is silent and discreet—carried out by the Secretary-General and his efficient collaborators. We therefore attach special importance to the assistance that the Latin American States may receive under the provisions of this paragraph.

Having concluded consideration of the specific provisions of the joint draft resolution, I should like to make three comments of a general nature on the draft itself, before going on to the third section of my statement.

1. The term "denuclearization" as used in the joint draft resolution means—and I think this is clear from the text of the declaration of the five Latin American presidents cited in the draft—prohibition of the existence of nuclear weapons and devices for launching of such weapons. Obviously, that prohibition does not extend to nuclear energy when used for peaceful purposes, which, on the contrary, can be of incalculable benefit in accelerating the development of the Latin American countries.

2. In five different parts of the draft, the words "Latin America" appear. In the constant exchange of views among the co-sponsors and other delegations, it has become evident that we must define the scope of these words; that is, we must set the geographical boundaries of what, for the purposes of the resolution, should be understood by "Latin America." I am sure, however, that everyone realizes the complexity of this matter and the careful studies that will be needed in order to reach an adequate solution. It would therefore be impossible to try to answer the question at this moment. That will be one of the tasks of the forthcoming Latin American conference on the denuclearization of the region. Nevertheless, I should like to state here and now that when the moment arrives for defining these boundaries, the Mexican delegation will insist on the inclusion of both Jamaica and Trinidad and Tobago, two new members of the United Nations whose territories are in the

Western Hemisphere. These two nations already have explicitly expressed their desire to associate with the states traditionally known as "Latin American" in their enterprise for denuclearization.

3. Furthermore, I should like to state in advance that the co-sponsors of the draft propose that measures of verification and inspection be adopted simultaneously with establishment of the denuclearized zone. But even though this question can now be answered affirmatively, I am sure that, as in the previous case, the members of the Committee will understand that, for the moment, it would be premature to go further. This will undoubtedly be another of the items that will appear on the agenda of the coming conference and it will require the greatest dedication and study. I might add only that the measures of verification must not run counter to the principle of non-intervention, rightly considered by Latin American states as the cornerstone of friendly relations among nations.

I have thus concluded the two main sections of my statement, leaving only the third and last section, which will be much shorter. As I indicated earlier, I shall refer to some aspects of the debate on the second item of the agenda of our Committee where direct or indirect mention was made of the topic that we have begun to discuss today.

I was surprised that several of the representatives, after recognizing that the establishment of a nuclear-free zone was primarily within the competence of the countries composing the zone, went on to enumerate a relatively long list of conditions, many of them impossible of fulfillment, which they believed to be indispensable to the creation of a nuclear-free zone.

Because the application of this procedure on a general and indiscriminate basis would in practice nullify the will expressed by states composing the zone and therefore would be contrary to recognition of that will as a decisive factor, and because, on the other hand, such an attitude would seem to forget that the United Nations, in Chapter I of its Charter, expressly grants the "sovereign equality of all its Members," I am inclined to believe that the intention of these speakers was chiefly to enumerate the conditions which they consider indispensable for an eventual denuclearization of the geographical zones in which their own countries are located.

Nevertheless, in view of the importance to be attached to the juridical aspect—and Mexico is a country which firmly believes with Benito Juárez that "peace is respect for the rights of others"—I should like to make some general comments that will serve to define the point of view of our delegation on this matter.

In order to avoid any ambiguity, I shall begin by pointing out that the geographical area in question is commonly known as "Latin

America." This zone enjoys a privileged position because it neither possesses nor wishes to possess nuclear weapons. Furthermore, Latin America does not form part nor does it desire to form part of the so-called balance of power or strategic balance of the world which others, perhaps more aptly, have called the balance of terror. We believe that in this area, which has still to be precisely defined on the maps, three types of denuclearized zones could be set up:

1. A nuclear-free zone that would cover all states and territories included in the area under discussion. This zone, which would be the idea envisaged by the Declaration of the five Latin American presidents and by the joint draft resolution A/C.1/L.329, could be established only if all the states composing the zone freely consent to their denuclearization.

2. A zone that embraces the territory of several states, neighboring or not, which, exercising their sovereign rights, undertake "not to manufacture, receive, store, or test nuclear weapons or nuclear launching devices."

3. A zone that contains only the territory of one state whose government has decided that in the interest of its people it should pass a law or decree whereby it unilaterally assumes this commitment.

My delegation believes that a denuclearized Latin American zone falling within either of the first two hypotheses would acquire juridical validity simply by virtue of the governments competent to take the decisions in each case signing the agreements or treaties in the free exercise of their sovereign rights.

Similarly, in the case of the third hypothesis or the denuclearization of a single state, it is enough that the necessary law or decree enter into force. I am sure that no one will challenge the right of a government to prohibit the planting of narcotics in its territory. It is, then, certainly competent to exclude nuclear weapons, which can be infinitely more destructive to its people than the most dangerous narcotic.

It is equally obvious that the other two hypotheses fall exclusively within the jurisdiction of the states directly concerned. In this connection, may I repeat what the representative of Ecuador said so aptly a few days ago:

The capacity of signing bilateral or multilateral agreements belongs exclusively to States; the sole limitation is that imposed by Article 103 of the Charter. The United Nations has no tutelary power over States; rather, it has the moral obligation to assist States in fulfilling the purposes and principles of the Charter, recommending any agreements that might alleviate international tensions and avoid the danger of widening conflicts.[9]

[9] United Nations Doc. A/C.1/PV.1328, 5 Nov. 1963.

15

I would go even further and add that the "moral obligation" referred to by Ambassador Benítez extends not only to our Organization but also to all the other states, including the nuclear Powers. We must, in effect, bear in mind that the main objective of establishing a denuclearized zone is to carry out a collateral measure of disarmament preventing the diffusion or proliferation of nuclear weapons. This has been the objective often and vigorously recommended by the General Assembly of the United Nations in its resolutions, which must be considered morally binding on the member states.

Having made clear the juridical aspect which my delegation attaches to this matter, we realize that in the circumstances of the world today the denuclearized zone cannot become fully effective unless the nuclear powers expressly undertake to respect the juridical statute which the state or states have freely decided on.

But it must also be unequivocally stated that a nuclear power that does not respect the juridical statute of denuclearization set up by a state or a group of states in the normal exercise of their sovereign rights would not only be violating a moral obligation but also a juridical obligation; namely, that assumed in the Charter of the United Nations when these countries solemnly bound themselves to refrain "from the threat or use of force against the territorial integrity or political independence of any state, or in any other manner inconsistent with the Purposes of the United Nations." It is obvious that only by means of force could the possession of nuclear weapons be imposed on a state or group of states which have decided not to permit the entry of such weapons into their territories.

I shall add that, in my opinion, this possibility can be discarded as far as Latin America is concerned; on the contrary, everything indicates that there will be no difficulty in achieving "at the appropriate moment" the "cooperation" mentioned with such confidence in operative paragraph 3 of the joint draft resolution.

To conclude, may I emphasize that the joint draft resolution of the ten Latin American countries, which the Mexican delegation has the honor of co-sponsoring, pursues a well-defined aim whose beneficial effects may, in the long run, be incalculable to Latin America and whose importance to its people would be difficult to exaggerate.

Notwithstanding all this, the immediate scope of the draft resolution is modest, because we are convinced of the need to proceed by stages, to make haste slowly as advised by the old Latin proverb. At the beginning of the general debate in the plenary, Dr. Araujo Castro pointed out:

With regard to the denuclearization of Latin America, my delegation, which has submitted this question as a specific item on the agenda, would like to

16

indicate that we are not proposing that Latin America be declared a denuclearized zone by the General Assembly. Brazil proposes that Latin American nations, as sovereign nations, should consider the possibility, by the most appropriate ways and means, of concluding a treaty under which they would commit themselves not to manufacture, store, receive, or test nuclear weapons. This is the sense which we attach to the proposal of the five Latin American countries, recently reaffirmed by a joint declaration of 30 April, signed by the Presidents of Bolivia, Brazil, Chile, Ecuador, and Mexico.[10]

To repeat the same idea in different words, I would add that the only purpose of the draft resolution is to give the General Assembly moral encouragement in its studies leading to the establishment of a regional "nuclear-free club" that may pave the way to the worldwide "nuclear-free club" foreseen by the former Minister of Foreign Affairs of Sweden, Mr. Unden. This enterprise actually is only the start of the gradual implementation of the plan to prevent the proliferation of nuclear arms, which has been unflaggingly supported by the Minister of Foreign Affairs of Ireland, Mr. Aiken.

Inasmuch as the United Nations has endorsed this noble proposal in so many of its resolutions, we dare hope that the First Committee and in due course the General Assembly will give our draft resolution the same unanimous support that two years ago it gave to Resolution 1665 (XVI) entitled "Prevention of the wider dissemination of nuclear weapons."

[10] GAOR: 18th Sess., 1208th Plenary Mtg., 19 Sept. 1963.

2 Speech Delivered at the 1265th
Plenary Meeting of the General Assembly of
the United Nations • on 27 November 1963

The resolution on the denuclearization of Latin America, which the General Assembly of the United Nations has just approved by the vote of an impressive majority of the member states and without a single negative vote, is at the same time a challenge and a testimony.

It is a challenge to the ability of Latin American states to work together and achieve unanimous results reflecting the intense desire for peace that is certainly felt by all its peoples. The Assembly has today successfully completed its work in the present session on this item on its agenda. It has given its wholehearted encouragement and moral support to the initiative of the five Latin American heads of state embodied in the Joint Declaration of 29 April 1963. In the resolution which we have just adopted, it "notes with satisfaction" this initiative and expresses the hope that the Latin American states will begin studies "concerning the measures that should be agreed upon with a view to achieving the aims of the said declaration." But the most difficult part of the task of carrying out the noble enterprise of denuclearization is still to be realized. It is the duty of the governments of the Latin American republics to begin this task without delay.

Whereas the resolution represents a challenge, it also constitutes a testimony that Latin America has now come of age and is able to assess correctly the real aspirations of its peoples. At the economic level, the Latin American Free Trade Association has already been created through the joint efforts of the Latin American countries, and I am

18

confident that in the not too distant future we shall see the birth of another Latin American association, designed to proscribe forever nuclear weapons from all the territories within the area whose limits we shall have to define.

It is a tribute to the political maturity of our peoples and governments that the resolution we have just adopted was drawn up entirely by the Latin American states and that it has received the unconditional support of eighteen of these states; furthermore, in our opinion, the abstention of the two remaining states can by no means be interpreted as excluding ultimate unanimity.

It shows clearly that we know what we want and that we shall know how to achieve it. We want to help make it possible for our children to grow up free from the terror inspired by the threat of nuclear war. We want to make sure that no part of Latin America will ever be used for testing nuclear weapons, no matter how or where the tests might be carried out. We want to eliminate even the slightest possibility that the scarce resources that we have available for developing our countries and raising the living standard of our peoples might be wasted in a ruinous and manifestly absurd nuclear armaments race. We want all states, and especially the nuclear powers, to agree to respect strictly, in all its aspects and consequences, the legal instrument on the denuclearization of Latin America which we may come to adopt. We want this question, as we have said from the beginning, to remain outside the so-called "cold war," which we still hope may have entered a final thaw thanks to the Moscow Treaty.

What is at stake is of the utmost importance. It involves the very life of present and future generations of Latin Americans, as is stated in the resolution adopted today. No one can evade responsibility before history for his conduct in this common task that is essential if such lofty objectives are to be attained.

We are keenly aware of the complexity and magnitude of the task before us; we must achieve a multilateral agreement which, in the first place, will fully satisfy the states of the region and the states that are concerned in any way with territories in this region, and which, in the second place, will satisfy the nuclear powers even though their interests are often in conflict.

We are confident, nevertheless, that in the not too distant future the Latin American states can bring an agreement before the Assembly. As President López Mateos said in his memorable letter of 21 March 1963: "It is true that the difficulties before us are great, but I believe—and I base this belief on our experience as peace-loving nations—that our will and ability to overcome them are equally great."

We do not intend to act rashly or hastily. We shall make haste slowly, as advised by the old Latin proverb, but we shall make haste.

Today, with the historic resolution adopted by this Assembly, Latin America starts along the road to denuclearization. And we are convinced that sooner or later we shall attain that goal, because we can count on the unqualified and enthusiastic support of all our peoples.

3 Speech Delivered at the Opening Meeting of the Preliminary Meeting on the Denuclearization of Latin America ▪ on 23 November 1964

As chairman of this Assembly, an honor generously bestowed on me by the distinguished representatives of the participating Latin American Republics, allow me to express not only my sincere gratitude for this signal honor, but also my interpretation of it as a tribute to Mexico for its unflagging and selfless work in behalf of the denuclearization of Latin America, which is the subject this Preliminary Meeting will discuss.

As the President of my country, Adolfo López Mateos, said on 21 March 1963 when he took the initiative for the preparation of a Joint Declaration on the denuclearization of Latin America, "this matter is linked to the welfare of this region of the world in which we live," and it is an enterprise that can be carried out ideally by "Latin America, which has so distinguished itself for its valuable contribution to the development of the great principles of law and justice."

The transcendence of the task which we shall undertake in this Meeting can best be appreciated by my commenting briefly on some of the provisions of Resolution 1911 (XVIII), entitled "Denuclearization of Latin America," which the General Assembly of the United Nations adopted almost a year ago today, on 27 November 1963, with the affirmative vote of all the states here represented.

As you will recall, in the first paragraph of the preamble of the resolution, the organ that fully represents the world organization stressed "the vital necessity of sparing present and future generations the scourge of a nuclear war."

A nuclear war. Three words that take scarcely a second to say, but which signify a potential catastrophe of terrifying and incalculable consequences for all mankind. I shall not resort to the fantastic lucubrations of what is generally known as science fiction, but to the respected voice of one of the greatest presidents the United States of America has known, the late John F. Kennedy. In his address to the General Assembly of the United Nations on 25 September 1961, he stated:

> For a nuclear disaster, spread by winds and water and fear, could well engulf the great and the small, the rich and the poor, the committed and the uncommitted alike. Mankind must put an end to war, or war will put an end to mankind. . . . And we in this Hall shall be remembered either as part of the generation that turned this planet into a flaming funeral pyre or as the generation that met its vow to "save succeeding generations from the scourge of war". . . . Together we shall save our planet—or together we shall perish in its flames.[11]

As a complement to this opinion, which acquires particular significance because it was expressed by someone who was not only a great president, but the president of the mightiest nuclear power of our time, it may be worth repeating some of the conclusions of experts concerning the destructive force of nuclear bombs. A single bomb of twenty-five megatons, for example—and it should not be forgotten that bombs of up to 100 megatons have already been tested—equals 25 million tons of explosives, or more than twelve times the total of all the bombings that were carried out in the Second World War, including the two atomic bombs dropped on Hiroshima and Nagasaki. The explosion of one such bomb would instantly destroy all life within a radius of eleven miles, without taking into account the subsequent effects, often fatal, of radioactive fallout.

I should also like to comment on another proposal of Resolution 1911: the text of the final paragraph of the preamble, which recognizes "the need to preserve, in Latin America, conditions which will prevent the countries of the region from becoming involved in a dangerous and ruinous arms race."

Until now, the Latin American republics have enjoyed and enjoy the privileged situation of not possessing nuclear weapons. For this reason, they have been spared the huge price of such weapons, a price that can be calculated if it is recalled that the cost of the first atomic bomb known to the world, which was exploded as an experiment in

[11] GAOR: 16th Sess., 1013rd Plenary Mtg.

Alamogordo, came to $2 billion. It would be a cruel mockery if to-morrow our countries were to divert to the purchase of nuclear weapons the meager resources they have available for improving the education, food, housing, and health of their peoples.

The information compiled by the United Nations and its specialized agencies highlights the enormous and urgent needs of this type which Latin America faces. Forty per cent of the adult population is illiterate. It has been estimated that from 1960 to 1970 more than $11 billion must be spent in order to provide adequate education. In 1960, 22 per cent of the population between five and fourteen years of age lacked scholastic opportunities, and at present about 6 million children do not receive an elementary education, while a secondary or higher educa-tion is beyond the reach of a large majority of the Latin American population. It is common knowledge that food, housing, and public health in Latin America are similarly deficient.

The foregoing observations may help us to appreciate the importance of studying, as the General Assembly hoped we would, "the measures that should be agreed upon with a view to achieving the aims" of the Declaration of 29 April 1963. They also make apparent the value of our efforts to hasten the day when it will be possible to conclude, as is provided in the Declaration, a multilateral Latin America agreement whereby the countries undertake not to manufacture, receive, store, or test nuclear weapons or nuclear launching devices.

We should not try to deceive ourselves by ignoring the complexity and magnitude of the task before us of achieving a multilateral agree-ment that will not only fully satisfy the states of the region and those states that are concerned with territories in this region, but will also permit the nuclear powers to "lend their full co-operation for the effective realization of the peaceful aims" inspiring Resolution 1911, as provided in paragraph 3 of this Resolution.

We are, nonetheless, confident that we are equal to the task, and we dare to hope that both the peoples and the governments of Latin America share the aims implicit in Resolution 1911. On 27 November 1963, the date of the historic meeting of the General Assembly at which this resolution was adopted, I synthesized these aims in the following terms:

We want to help make it possible for our children to grow up free from the terror inspired by the threat of nuclear war.

We want to make sure that no part of Latin America will ever be used for testing nuclear weapons, no matter how or where the tests might be carried out.

We want to eliminate even the slightest possibility that the scarce resources that we have available for developing our countries and the living standard of our peoples might be wasted in a ruinous and manifestly absurd nuclear armaments race.

We want all states, and especially the nuclear powers, to agree to respect strictly, in all its aspects and consequences, the legal instrument on the denuclearization of Latin America which we may come to adopt.

We want this question, as we have said from the beginning, to remain outside the so-called "cold war," which we still hope may have entered a final thaw thanks to the Moscow Treaty.

We are convinced that the discussions that we begin today, in spite of the brevity of this Preliminary Meeting, will be very constructive and fruitful, especially if they are directed, on the one hand, toward an attempt to specify the problems that will have to be solved by subsequent studies and, on the other, toward an agreement on the most appropriate method to carry out such studies with the necessary continuity and effectiveness.

In this connection, I should like to point out that, in our opinion, two specific problems that undoubtedly will require careful study, with a view to obtaining for them a unanimous solution, are to define the geographical limits of what, for the purposes of the multilateral treaty, should be understood by "Latin America," and to establish the methods of verification, inspection, and control that should be adopted to ensure the faithful fulfillment of the obligations contracted under the treaty.

The other aspect, the continuity of studies to be carried out after the Preliminary Meeting, can be best ensured by setting up at the end of the Meeting a kind of "preparatory commission," which we would instruct to work intensively on the solution of the problems outlined above.

I am sure that in the course of our discussions all the distinguished delegates to this Meeting can contribute valuable ideas and suggestions for realizing the aspirations of the 91 states, including those represented here, which voted for Resolution 1911—a resolution that, as you know, did not receive a single negative vote.

To conclude, permit me to extend to you a cordial welcome in the name of the government of my country. We hope that you will find here a suitable setting for the work we begin today. Mexico's position on disarmament is well known, as are its unremitting efforts to forge an era of peace based on law, justice, equal rights, and mutual respect, in which the legal postulate of the sovereign equality of all states would be duly recognized in the daily reality of international relations.

The independent policy of Mexico in international affairs is not subject to fortuitous or circumstantial conditions; because it arises naturally and spontaneously from our historic past, its continuity is guaranteed. In this respect, the statements made by President López Mateos when he announced his initiative for the denuclearization of Latin America, which I quoted earlier, may appropriately be accompanied by the words of the President-elect of Mexico when he accepted his nomination as presidential candidate on 17 November 1963. On that occasion, Gustavo Díaz Ordaz made a statement that is very relevant to the task we have before us:

We struggle for peace in the knowledge that the self-destruction of mankind is today not a remote possibility but one that we must contend with; we support disarmament, beginning with denuclearization, for we are convinced that either the world puts an end to nuclear weapons, or nuclear weapons will put an end to the world.[12]

---

[12] Gustavo Diaz Ordaz, *Pensamiento Politico* (Mexico, 1964), Vol. I, p. 17.

4 Speech Delivered at the Closing Meeting of the Preliminary Meeting on the Denuclearization of Latin America ▪ on 27 November 1964

By a happy coincidence our meeting is going to close on the very date on which, one year ago, the General Assembly of the United Nations adopted its Resolution 1911 (XVIII) on the denuclearization of Latin America.

I am convinced that we have commemorated this splendid anniversary in the best way possible by approving the resolution on "Establishment of a Preparatory Commission for the Denuclearization of Latin America," which appears as section II in the Final Act and which charges this Commission with the transcendental task of preparing a preliminary draft of a multilateral treaty for the denuclearization of Latin America.

Simón Bolívar initiated the Congress of Panama held in 1826 by circulating an invitation which stated: "One hundred centuries from now, when posterity traces the origin of our public law back to the treaties that shaped its future, it will honor the Isthmus protocols. There, in the first alliances, it will find the design of our future relations with the world. What then will the Isthmus of Corinth be next to that of Panama?"

Without resorting to the extravagant language that was so popular in the nineteenth century, I believe that we can justifiably state that when the coming generations of Latin America look for the origin of the noble enterprise that banished the threat of nuclear devastation from their homeland, they will accord equal honor to three basic documents: the Joint Declaration of 29 April 1963; Resolution 1911 (XVIII) of the United Nations; and the Resolution that we have just approved unanimously, which is section II in the Final Act of this Meeting. The first two contain the underlying principles and the third contains the birth certificate of the institution. Together, these documents should make possible the denuclearization of Latin America; that is, the proscription of all nuclear weapons and launching devices from the Latin American continent.

Therefore, distinguished representatives, I firmly believe that, as the Preliminary Meeting on the Denuclearization of Latin America closes, we can all be satisfied that we have carried out a task, apparently modest, but of incalculable significance. We have worked for the benefit of not only our own countries and of Latin America but also, in this world of interdependence in which we live, for the good of mankind.

5 Speech Delivered at the Opening Meeting of the First Session of the Preparatory Commission for the Denuclearization of Latin America ▪ on 15 March 1965

At an international conference it is customary for the head of the delegation of the host country to preside over the conference. This tradition, together with the generosity of the distinguished representatives gathered here—for which, of course, I am deeply grateful—explains the signal honor conferred upon me by my designation as chairman of the Preparatory Commission for the Denuclearization of Latin America, an honor I also enjoyed at the Preliminary Meeting held here from 23 to 27 November 1964. I shall do everything within my power to justify the confidence implied by this appointment.

After conveying to you the wishes of the President of Mexico, Gustavo Díaz Ordaz, as well as of the Minister of Foreign Affairs, Antonio Carrillo Flores, for the success of the Commission, I should like to make a brief summary of some facts that should be borne in mind because they are intimately linked with the task that we are about to undertake. Inasmuch as I am sure that all the members of the Commission are familiar with the background of the case, I shall save time by not reviewing the Joint Declaration of 29 April 1963 by the five Latin American heads of state on the initiative of the President of Mexico, Adolfo López Mateos; for the same reason, I need not recall Resolution 1911 (XVIII), which the General Assembly of the United Nations adopted without a single negative vote on 27 November 1963.

I shall limit myself to a few general comments on the results of the Preliminary Meeting of November 1964 and to a discussion of some of the main points of the two resolutions that appear at the beginning of the Final Act of the meeting.

First, I shall express my conviction that the states participating in the Preliminary Meeting, all of whom belong to the Preparatory Commission, can feel entirely satisfied with the results achieved at that time which, I am equally sure, will greatly expedite the work of this Commission.

The Preliminary Meeting began by defining the meaning and scope of the term "denuclearization" in a way that would prevent any misinterpretation of the objective that is pursued. In its Resolution I, entitled "Reaffirmation of the proposed denuclearization of Latin America," the Preliminary Meeting declared "that for the purposes of the Meeting 'denuclearization' shall mean the absence of nuclear weapons and nuclear launching devices"; at the same time that it decided "to reaffirm the aims set forth in the joint Declaration of 29 April 1963 and ratified in resolution 1911 (XVIII) of the United Nations General Assembly," it stressed "the advisability of promoting international cooperation for the peaceful use of nuclear energy, especially for the benefit of the developing countries."

Resolution II may be considered just as important as the first resolution and, in some ways, even more so. It enabled the Meeting to act as a constitutent assembly which not only created the Preparatory Commission and designated its membership and headquarters, but also clearly and precisely defined the aim of the Commission while simultaneously outlining the procedures to be followed in order to achieve this aim. The Meeting, furthermore, made a series of wise recommendations to ensure the success of these procedures. In other words, it concerned itself not only with the objective we all desire, but also with the most appropriate means to realize this objective.

I believe that at this time nothing can contribute more to expedite our work than to bear in mind the provisions of Resolution II of the Preliminary Meeting. In the first place, this resolution clearly instructs the Commission "to prepare a preliminary draft of a multilateral treaty for the denuclearization of Latin America and, to this end, to undertake the preparatory studies and measures which it considers appropriate." The resolution is equally precise in setting forth the methods that should be used:

The Commission shall constitute from its membership the working groups which it deems necessary and which shall perform their functions either at the headquarters of the Commission or elsewhere, as appropriate, and a committee to coordinate their work, to be called the "Coordinating Committee."

29

Resolution II recommends that the Preparatory Commission give priority in its work to matters that I believe are sufficiently important to list once again:

(a) the definition of the geographical boundaries of the area to which the treaty should apply;

(b) the methods of verification, inspection, and control that should be adopted to ensure the faithful fulfillment of the obligations contracted under the treaty;

(c) action designed to secure the collaboration in the Commission's work of the Latin American republics that were not represented at the Preliminary Meeting;

(d) action designed to ensure that the extra-continental or continental states which, in addition to the Latin American republics, exercise *de jure* or *de facto* international responsibility for territories situated within the boundaries of the geographical area to which the treaty applies, agree to contract the same obligations with regard to these territories as the above-mentioned republics contract with regard to their own;

(e) action designed to obtain from the nuclear powers a commitment to the effect that they will strictly respect the legal instrument on the denuclearization of Latin America as regards all its aspects and consequences.

This is certainly not a complete list—and the text of Resolution II makes clear that the Preliminary Meeting did not try to make it complete—of the numerous and complex matters that the Preparatory Commission will have to study. But it is also unquestionable that the above-listed matters are of a transcendence that amply justified the Meeting in recommending that they be given priority.

Another of the conclusions that may be drawn from the foregoing is that at some time during this First Session the Commission will have to study and resolve the question of the working groups that it may wish to set up in addition to the Coordinating Committee, and of the terms of reference of these organs.

In the same connection, it is well to recall the provisions of paragraph 4 of Resolution 1911 (XVIII) of the General Assembly of the United Nations, wherein the General Assembly itself requested "the Secretary-General to extend to the States of Latin America, at their request, such technical facilities as they may require in order to achieve the aims set forth" in this resolution. Clearly, the use of these technical facilities may be invaluable with regard to many aspects of our difficult undertaking. Thanks to its long association with the work of the Eighteen-Nation Committee on Disarmament, the Secretariat of the

United Nations now constitutes the most important repository of knowledge and experience on the subject.

I do not want to finish without first saying a few words about the enormous responsibility that our peoples and governments have conferred on us by appointing us to represent them in this Preparatory Commission for the Denuclearization of Latin America, an enterprise which, if we can carry it to a successful conclusion, will go beyond the regional sphere and will exert a healthy influence on the world at large by offering mankind the first example of a multilateral treaty to proscribe nuclear weapons. Our task involves, as on another occasion I declared before the General Assembly of the United Nations, not only a challenge but evidence of the maturity of Latin America.

In the introduction to his last Annual Report, U Thant, Secretary-General of the United Nations, stated: "Another area where progress is most urgent is in the prevention of the spread of nuclear weapons."[13]

During the first part of the nineteenth session of the General Assembly, held from last December to February of this year, many representatives of countries all over the world, either in conversations or in formal statements in the general debates of the Assembly, gave high praise to the work that the states today represented here have been carrying out for the denuclearization of Latin America.

I shall cite only the statement made by the distinguished Minister of Foreign Affairs of Sweden in the general debate of 22 January. Chancellor Torsten Nilsson, after pointing out that "the present moment seems to be propitious for concerted and energetic attempts to reach a broad agreement on a freeze of nuclear armaments" and that "the demands for international action in order to halt the further proliferation of nuclear weapons have been given new impetus and taken on added strength," referred specifically to the efforts of the African states to achieve the denuclearization of their continent, and he had this praise for the Latin American states:

At the same time, the Latin American countries represented at the meeting in Mexico City in November of last year have brought to our attention their decision to initiate detailed studies on a treaty for the denuclearization of Latin America. They have already given us valuable definitions of the aims and scope of such a treaty.

The Swedish Government attaches special importance to these attempts at organizing regional co-operation in order to reduce the nuclear peril that hangs over mankind. If groups of countries, in areas where conditions for such arrangements exist, were to freeze the nuclear situation by regional agreements, the cause of peace and disarmament would be well served.[14]

13 United Nations Doc. A/5801/Add.1, 18 Nov. 1964.
14 United Nations Doc. A/PV. 1319, 22 Jan. 1965.

The third example illustrating the importance of denuclearization in general and in Latin America specifically is furnished by the words of Hubert Humphrey, Vice-President of the United States of America, one of the leading nuclear powers in the world. In a recent speech in New York on 17 February, he stated:

If the need for preventing the proliferation of nuclear weapons is more immediate in Asia today, it is no less important in Latin America, Africa, and the Near East. All of these areas are ripe for regional arms pacts which would prevent these countries from developing nuclear weapons. Nuclear weapons would serve no useful purpose in preserving their security. The introduction of these weapons would provoke a rivalry that would imperil the peace of Latin America and Africa and intensify the present rivalries in the Near East. It would endanger the precarious economies of countries which already possess military forces too large for their security needs and too expensive to be maintained without outside assistance.

Such nuclear arms control agreements should naturally be initiated by the nations of the area. In Latin America, such an agreement has already been proposed. Should the nations of Latin America, of Africa, and the Near East, through their own institutions or through the United Nations, take the initiative in establishing nuclear free zones, they will earn the appreciation of all nations of the world. Containment in these areas would represent a major step toward world peace.[15]

At the opening meeting of the Preliminary Meeting on the Denuclearization of Latin America on 23 November 1964, I quoted the words used by the President of Mexico in his speech of acceptance one year earlier as candidate to the Presidency. He declared that denuclearization is a task that cannot be postponed, for we find ourselves faced with a fatal dilemma: "either the world puts an end to nuclear weapons or nuclear weapons will put an end to the world."

Let me conclude today by again quoting President Díaz Ordaz. At his inauguration as President on 1 December 1964, he made the following statement:

Not only the highest idealism but the most elementary common sense dictates the defense of peace, because today this is a requisite for man's survival.

To desire peace is to oppose the conditions that make war possible. We support disarmament, beginning with denuclearization. We maintain that peace will be assured only so far as conditions are created that will make all peoples determined to consolidate it.[16]

---

[15] United States Mission to the United Nations, Press Release No. 4500.
[16] *México de Hoy*, No. 170 (December 1964), p. 198.

6 Speech Delivered at the Closing Meeting of the First Session of the Preparatory Commission for the Denuclearization of Latin America ▪ on 22 March 1965

Today we have reached the end of the first stage of the work of the Preparatory Commission for the Denuclearization of Latin America. The road ahead of us is neither short nor easy, but we should take heart as much from what we have accomplished—which is not inconsiderable—as from the fact that all the resolutions adopted at this time, like those adopted at the Preliminary Meeting of November 1964, have been approved unanimously.

As in ancient Greece and in the Olympics of today, we pass the torch to the three working groups that we have set up. We trust that in five months we shall receive it back from them, its flame renewed, in this relay race which we have undertaken and upon which, we can say without exaggeration, depend the fate and even the life of the future genrations of Latin America.

These working groups have been set up in the most favorable conditions to successfully conclude the task that has been entrusted to them, not only because of their membership but because of the precise definition of their terms of reference. They also have available at all times the technical facilities of the Secretariat of the United Nations, which is at present the most important repository of knowledge and experience in matters related to denuclearization and disarmament in general.

If I were to make some recommendation to the working groups in my capacity as chairman of the Preparatory Commission, it would be only that they should never lose sight of the final objective of our Commission, which is clearly stated in Resolution II of the Preliminary Meeting: the preparation of a multilateral treaty for the denuclearization of Latin America.

In the light of the results already obtained, it seems reasonable to expect that this preliminary draft may in due time be approved by the unanimous vote of the members of the Commission and that the latter may eventually embrace—as it almost does now—all the Latin American republics.

We still cannot predict when or how we shall manage to accomplish the denuclearization of Latin America, that is, to make the privileged nuclear-free situation of our countries permanent and, consequently, to proscribe forever from their territories nuclear weapons and nuclear launching devices.

But we can, and I am convinced of this, state that the denuclearization of Latin America will sooner or later become a reality because it has been given the wholehearted and enthusiastic support of the Latin American peoples.

Thus, on concluding our work for this first session, it seems to me unnecessary to express my hope for an outcome that, as I have stated, I consider inevitable. But I do hope that our Commission may carry out its work in such a way that, in the not too distant future, the desired objective may be achieved by using a procedure which, although not the only one possible, would undoubtedly be the most suitable: a treaty for the denuclearization of our America that bears the signatures, without any reservation, of the representatives of the twenty republics that traditionally have constituted Latin America.

7 Speech Delivered at the Opening Meeting of the Second Session of the Preparatory Commission for the Denuclearization of Latin America ▪ on 23 August 1965

I can think of no better way to begin the work of the second session of the Preparatory Commission for the Denuclearization of Latin America than the way in which I opened the first session of this same Commission; namely, to present a rapid review of what has been accomplished, so that we can not only evaluate these results, but also have a good idea of what remains to be done.

At the risk of appearing redundant, I wish first to recall that from the beginning of their work the Latin American republics stated their purpose clearly and unequivocally. This purpose was already defined in the first of the resolutions approved by the Preliminary Meeting on the Denuclearization of Latin America on 27 November 1964, the anniversary of the adoption of Resolution 1911 (XVIII) by the General Assembly of the United Nations. The former resolution established that "denuclearization," with regard to the Latin American territories, should be taken to mean "the absence of nuclear weapons and nuclear launching devices." In other words, the governments of the Latin American republics, reflecting the legitimate aspirations and desires of their peoples, endeavour to guarantee with the treaty whose preliminary draft will be prepared by our Commission, the absolute proscription of nuclear weapons and nuclear launching devices, no matter what state may control them, from the territories covered by this instrument.

The objective is to keep Latin America free forever, as it has fortunately been until now, of nuclear weapons and launching devices.

We are well aware that the privileged circumstances existing in Latin America are not duplicated in some other regions. We do not seek, therefore, to impose the system of Latin American denuclearization either as a model for universal application or even as a precedent. I am sure that all the states here represented will study with an open and constructive spirit the proposals of universal scope that may be considered in the sphere of the United Nations. But we are firmly convinced that for the Latin American peoples only the system of "absence," already solemnly proclaimed, can be acceptable. This is a crystal-clear concept, which does not permit erroneous or subtle interpretations, and which can mean nothing but the non-existence, in perpetuity, of nuclear weapons.

In the five months that have passed since the first session of the Commission set up the Coordinating Committee and the three Working Groups, the work carried out by these subsidiary organs proves the correctness of the decisions which led to their establishment. This plenary owes a debt of gratitude to each and every one of their members for the valuable information which they have submitted to the Commission.

In addition to the constructive agreements and proposals of the Coordinating Committee and the reports of Working Groups A and C, the Commission has before it in its present session document COPRE-DAL/GB/DT/1 submitted by Working Group B, which contains the preliminary draft of the fourteen articles for the Treaty for the Denuclearization of Latin America relative to verification, inspection, and control. I hardly need to stress the significance of this document. It is the first time in the history of negotiations between states on disarmament, or such collateral measures of disarmament as denuclearization, that even at the level of a subsidiary organ, it has been possible to obtain unanimity on this question. Consensus has been achieved on a series of provisions aimed at overcoming what has been hitherto one of the main obstacles—if not the main one—to any agreement on disarmament.

It is not up to me, but to the Commission, to study carefully the proposals to which I have just referred. I wish only to say that it is my impression that the document in question, as a whole, meets the primary requisite, which I defined on 11 November 1963, when I participated in the discussions of the First Committee of the General Assembly of the United Nations. This requisite was that "there must not be the slightest risk that the measures of verification run counter to the principle of non-intervention, rightly considered by all Latin American

States as the cornerstone of friendly relations among nations".

I should like to draw the attention of the Commission to two other aspects: one is the important role that Working Group B assigns to the International Atomic Energy Agency, which comprises almost all the Latin American republics and which enjoys indisputable competence, authority, and moral stature; the other is the detailed rules included by the Working Group in its preliminary draft to make possible explosions of nuclear materials for peaceful purposes without risk of violation or impairment of the obligations undertaken under the treaty.

I cannot end these brief comments without expressing the Commission's gratitude to the Secretary-General of the United Nations, His Excellency U Thant, for making possible the accomplishment of Working Group B by his collaboration, both in the form of specially prepared and selected information—which the Representatives have available in working paper COPREDAL/GB/S/2 Annex—and through the valuable services of Mr. William Epstein, Chief of the Disarmament Affairs Division of the United Nations Secretariat, who acted as technical adviser to Working Group B and who, in the same capacity, will be available to the Preparatory Commission during the present session.

Working Groups A and C, it will be recalled, were instructed, respectively, to take action designed to ensure that certain states undertake, with regard to territories under their international responsibility, the same obligations that are undertaken by the Latin American republics with respect to denuclearization (Group A); and to take action designed to obtain from the nuclear powers the commitment that they will strictly respect the legal instrument on the denuclearization of Latin America in all its aspects and consequences (Group C). It must be recognized that, in spite of the dedicated and praiseworthy efforts of their members, the work of these groups has not been as fruitful nor has it progressed as rapidly as that of Group B.

Nonetheless, I believe that this should not be a cause for discouragement and that continued negotiations with the duly authorized representatives of the states, and especially of the nuclear powers, cannot fail to yield in the near future the positive results that we all hope for. It should be borne in mind that many people officially connected with these powers have made openly favorable declarations either concerning the denuclearization of zones that are in the privileged position of Latin America—to which specific reference has been made in several speeches—or concerning the creation of denuclearized zones in general.

Allow me to quote, as examples, from some of these declarations.

In my opening speech at the first session, I referred to the ideas expressed on 17 February of this year by the Vice-President of the United States of America, Hubert Humphrey. Rather than repeat this quota-

37

tion in its entirety, I shall read once again only the last two sentences:

> Should the nations of Latin America, of Africa, and the Near East, through their own institutions, or through the United Nations, take the initiative in establishing nuclear-free zones, they will earn the appreciation of all nations of the world. Containment in these areas would represent a major step toward world peace.

Subsequently, Senator Robert F. Kennedy, speaking in the United States Senate exactly two months ago today, on 23 June, declared:

> Right now, one of our greatest assets is that there is not one nuclear weapon in all of Latin America or Africa. This situation can be preserved if the nuclear powers pledge not to introduce any nuclear weapons into these areas, the nations of the areas pledge not to acquire them, and appropriate machinery for the verification of these pledges is set up. Some nations—particularly Latin America—have already exchanged informal assurances to this effect. We should encourage them to go further in every possible way.[17]

As for the other great nuclear power, the Union of Soviet Socialist Republics, its representative in the First Committee of the General Assembly of the United Nations, Ambassador Federenko, on 30 October 1963 defined the attitude of his government in the following terms:

> Another effective measure to prevent the proliferation of nuclear weapons would be to conclude an agreement to prohibit the stationing and production of nuclear weapons in particular geographic zones, which might cover whole continents or specific countries. It is well known that in recent years many proposals have been made to create such zones almost all over the world. The Soviet Government believes that it is vital to help to put into practice these plans. We are prepared to join with the Western Powers in giving the necessary guarantees to keep nuclear weapons out of areas designated nuclear-free zones, whether through regional or multilateral agreements, or even through bilateral agreements if only one country wishes to declare its territory a nuclear-free zone.[18]

Still more recently, on 7 December 1964, the Minister of Foreign Affairs of the Soviet Union, Andrei Gromyko, presented to the General Assembly of the United Nations a memorandum which includes the following statements:

> The Soviet Government considers that, in the interests of strengthening peace and barring the spread of nuclear weapons, not only groups of States embracing whole continents or large geographical regions but also more

[17] United States, *Congressional Record*, 89th Congress, 1st Session, Vol. 111, No. 113, p. 14051.

[18] United Nations Doc. A/C.1/PV.1321, 30 October 1963.

limited groups of States and even individual countries may assume obligations for the establishment of denuclearized zones . . .

The Soviet Government is prepared to undertake an obligation to respect the status of all denuclearized zones that may be established, if the same obligation is assumed by other nuclear Powers as well.[19]

I believe that such categorical and authorized statements as those I have just cited justify a reasonable amount of optimism concerning the final result of our actions designed to obtain adequate guarantees from the nuclear powers on the Treaty for the Denuclearization of Latin America. It would not be logical to consider that such denuclearization "would represent a major step toward world peace" and that the Latin American republics should be encouraged "to go further in every possible way"; to consider it "vital to help put into practice these plans" for establishing denuclearized zones even "if only one country wishes to declare its territory a nuclear-free zone"; and at the same time to make effective support of the Latin American treaty depend on conditions that would either prevent or would delay indefinitely the granting of the requested guarantees.

We also dare to hope that another of the nuclear powers may modify its position—which is until now altogether negative according to the reports of Working Groups A and C. We would certainly be very sorry to see this attitude continued. Our peoples would not understand it in the light of the close historic ties as well as the cultural affinities that Latin America enjoys with the power concerned. Furthermore, the government of this power in recent years has stressed again and again the importance that it attaches—just as we do—to fostering relations with the Latin American republics, in the interest of progress and peace.

In addition to the reports of the Coordinating Committee and of the three groups, the Commission will receive for consideration a working paper prepared by the Secretariat—in accordance with the agreement to that effect adopted by the Coordinating Committee—which will help the Commission in its task of drawing up in this session the preamble of the preliminary draft of the treaty.

There is one final point on which I should like to make some general comments: the really incalculable importance of the results of the enterprise that we have undertaken, which can be appreciated by reflecting on the catastrophic consequences for all mankind of a nuclear conflagration. The prevailing opinion among leading scientists is that there are real possibilities that a great nuclear war would change man's plasma in such a way that the human species, as we know it, could not

[19] United Nations Doc. A/5827, 7 December 1964.

survive and that the radioactivity generated would eventually make the whole earth uninhabitable.

At the beginning of August Pope Paul VI with good reason described nuclear weapons as an "outrage to civilization"; urged once again the banning of "the terrible art that knows how to make these arms, to multiply and store them for the terror of peoples"; prayed that "that homicidal weapon may not have killed peace in the world, may not have injured forever the honor of science, and that it has not extinguished the serenity of life on this earth"; and emphasized that men must "no longer place their trust, their calculations, and their prestige in such fatal and dishonoring weapons."[20]

For the realization of such compelling objectives, regional denuclearization—even in the strictly technical sense of "absence of nuclear weapons" given to it by the Latin American republics—will certainly not be the decisive factor, but only a means. It is a means, however, that can give the difficult initial thrust to a movement that will become irresistible and that, as part of a coordinated disarmament plan, will culminate in what was unanimously approved in 1954 by the General Assembly of the United Nations in its Resolution 808 (IX): "the total prohibition of the use and manufacture of nuclear weapons and weapons of mass destruction of every type, together with the conversion of existing stocks of nuclear weapons for peaceful purposes."

A familiar proverb points out that tall oaks from little acorns grow. The denuclearization of Latin America may be one of these acorns; it may serve as an example for the denuclearization of other areas of the world, which are still fortunate enough not to have outside nuclear weapons in their territories. Denuclearization—or at least containment—can then be extended, from the moment that the directly interested countries consider it desirable, to states which, although they have outside nuclear weapons in their territories, still do not produce them. Once this exterior or extra-national proliferation is checked between countries or groups of countries, the next step—which has already received encouragement from some nuclear powers—will be to gradually reduce, until totally suspended, intra-national or internal proliferation; that is, what is produced through the steady manufacture of new nuclear weapons by the powers capable of doing so. This suspension could be followed by the gradual reduction of the reserves accumulated by the nuclear powers, which together with other analogous measures relative to "conventional weapons," would constitute a transcendental contribution to hastening the day when general and complete disarmament under effective control may become the reality aspired to by all the peoples of the world.

[20] *The New York Times,* 9 August 1965.

The denuclearization of Latin America is an end in itself in the sense that it brings manifest and inestimable benefits to present and future generations by preventing the Latin American countries from becoming the eventual target of nuclear attacks and by keeping the region out of a ruinous nuclear-armament race, which would divert to military purposes the limited resources available for economic development.

Furthermore, the effects of Latin American denuclearization, as I have just said, would be universal in scope. The importance and growing number of the states in other continents that have sent observers to follow the work of our Commission, and the increasingly frequent references to this work in international forums and in the foreign press are a clear indication that world opinion is convinced of this.

To conclude, I have only to say once again to the distinguished members of the Preparatory Commission gathered here that our work is wished every success both by the President of Mexico, Gustavo Díaz Ordaz—who, as you will recall, some time ago publicly stated his conviction that "either the world puts an end to nuclear weapons, or nuclear weapons will put an end to the world"—and by his Minister of Foreign Affairs, Antonio Carrillo Flores.

For myself, I need not repeat that as chairman of the Preparatory Commission, I shall continue to make every effort to achieve the objective assigned to this organ by the Latin American republics through their representatives: the preparation of a preliminary draft for the Treaty for the Denuclearization of Latin America in which an international agreement will be undertaken to maintain this region free forever, as is its privileged position today, from nuclear weapons and nuclear launching devices.

8 Speech Delivered at the Closing Meeting of the Second Session of the Preparatory Commission for the Denuclearization of Latin America ▪ on 2 September 1965

Once again we are going to part after a second period of continuous work in which we have in every way made more progress than in the first period.

With every justification, it seems to me, the Preparatory Commission has felt compelled, after taking stock of the results already obtained, to urge the governments of the member states, in its Resolution 10 (II), to redouble their efforts and to take every measure that they may deem appropriate to enable the Commission to draw up during its Third Session—which will convene at its headquarters on 19 April of next year—the preliminary draft of a treaty for the denuclearization of Latin America, in accordance with the instructions given to it by the Preliminary Meeting on the Denuclearization of Latin America in 1964.

With regard to the complex and delicate aspect of verification, inspection, and control, the Commission has been able to transmit to the governments, with legitimate satisfaction, the preliminary draft articles which, in the words of Resolution 9 (II), it has considered "with special appreciation." These articles will certainly represent an invaluable contribution in this matter, which, both because of its highly technical character and because of its political repercussions, constitutes one of the most difficult problems to be solved in order to conclude the treaty that we strive for.

Another aspect of the work of the Commission is to obtain, on the one hand, the agreement of the United States of America and of other extra-continental states to assume, in respect of certain territories situated in the Western Hemisphere, the same obligations that the Latin American republics undertake in respect of their own territories and, on the other, to obtain a commitment from the nuclear powers to strictly respect the legal instrument on the denuclearization of Latin America. The Commission, therefore, has set up a high-level Negotiating Committee which will try to accelerate the attainment of these objectives as much as possible.

One of the results—and not the least important by any means—of this Second Session of the Commission is its unanimous approval of a declaration of principles which, as Resolution 8 (II) establishes, should "serve as a basis for the Preamble of the preliminary draft of a Multilateral Treaty for the Denuclearization of Latin America." I am sure that the peoples of Latin America will consider that their governments faithfully interpret their desires and aspirations if this preamble is based on the concepts which are summarized at the end of the above document and which express the conviction of the governments:

That the denuclearization of the States represented at the Conference— being understood to mean the undertaking entered into internationally in this Treaty to keep their territories free forever, as they have been hitherto, from nuclear weapons and their launching devices—will constitute a measure of protection for their peoples against the squandering of their limited resources on nuclear armaments and against possible nuclear attacks upon their territories; a significant contribution towards preventing the proliferation of nuclear weapons; and a powerful factor for general and complete disarmament; and

That Latin America, faithful to its deep-seated tradition of universality of outlook, must endeavour not only to banish from its homelands the scourge of nuclear war, but also, at the same time, to cooperate in the fulfillment of the ideals of mankind, that is to say in the consolidation of a lasting peace based on equal rights, economic fairness and social justice for all, in accordance with the principles and purposes of the Charter of the United Nations. . . .

Although it deals with a procedural instrument, Resolution 6 (II) also deserves mention because it expresses the moving spirit of the Commission in the sense that "the documents of the Preparatory Commission and its subsidiary organs shall continue to be placed in general distribution unless, because of exceptional circumstances, the Commission or the competent subsidiary organ decides otherwise." Convinced of the nobleness and high principles of our aims, we have nothing to hide either from the press or other communication media, or from the public in general. We want, therefore, to carry out our work in full view.

In addition to the advances specifically recorded in resolutions, our debates have been extremely helpful in making clear some important aspects of the task before us. Thus, for example, it seems to me that an objective study of the records of our meetings reveals that, of the four possible alternatives listed in the report of Working Group A— presented to us by the distinguished Representatives of Ecuador, Ambassador Benites Vinueza, as Vice-Chairman and Rapporteur of the Group—for defining the geographical boundaries of the area to which the denuclearization treaty should be applied, a large majority, if not all, of the representatives who have spoken are in favor of the third alternative, namely, that the denuclearized area shall be automatically defined when the treaty enters into force or, in other words, that such an area shall equal the sum of the territories in which the treaty applies by virtue of the will of the governments ratifying the treaty.

There are, of course, different shades of opinion within this alternative, inasmuch as some representatives believe that the adherence of a particular state is essential; whereas other representatives have placed no conditions. But these different views—which we must make every effort to reconcile—in no way invalidate the conclusion I have drawn. It is probable that this general agreement, together with the results we can reasonably expect from the work of the Negotiating Committee, will solve one of the main problems that we have requested Working Group A to study.

While I am speaking about the Negotiating Committee, permit me to add that, as one of its members, I hope that the authorized representatives of the nuclear powers—with whom, on the instructions of the Commission, we are going to enter into conversations at United Nations Headquarters in New York City—will be willing to prove with deeds the positions they have maintained in Geneva in the Eighteen-Nation Committee on Disarmament. The first article of the "Draft Treaty to Prevent the Spread of Nuclear Weapons," submitted to this Committee on 17 August of this year by one of the leading nuclear powers, stipulates:

1) Each of the nuclear States Party to this Treaty undertakes not to transfer any nuclear weapons into the national control of any non-nuclear State, either directly, or indirectly through a military alliance, and each undertakes not to take any other action which would cause an increase in the total number of States and other organizations having independent power to use nuclear weapons.

2) Each of the nuclear states Party to this Treaty undertakes not to assist any non-nuclear State in the manufacture of nuclear weapons.[21]

This, and only this, is fundamentally the commitment that the Preparatory Commission wants to obtain from the nuclear powers with regard to Latin America, with the sole addition that their commitment should also cover the obligation not to permit, and still less to attempt, to impose in Latin America nuclear weapons under their control. This is a commitment that seems to us to be easy to agree to because it is certain, as far as it is humanly possible to be certain of anything, that at present no nuclear weapons exist in Latin American territory.

I also wish to cite what was recently said in the Disarmament Committee on 19 August by the representative of another of the nuclear powers. After quoting the prophetic words that Shakespeare puts into the mouth of Brutus in his tragedy devoted to Julius Caesar—"There is a tide in the affairs of men which, taken at the flood, leads on to fortune; omitted, all the voyage of their life is bound in shallows and in miseries"—this representative goes on to state with ample reason:

I believe, quite simply and without any wish to over-dramatize the dangers, that unless we can stop and set back the nuclear arms race before many more months have passed, we may have little to look forward to but shallows and miseries.

And I believe that the first thing we must do is stop nuclear weapons from spreading from country to country . . . It means that we are passing, quickly and perhaps irrevocably, beyond the point at which the spread of nuclear weapons can be stopped. If the non-nuclear powers of the world, and especially those that are non-aligned, cease to look upon nuclear weapons as an evil and begin to look upon them instead as a symbol of prestige and power, to be acquired or renounced simply on grounds of narrow national expediency, then we shall be lost.[22]

It seems to me that the eloquent speech that I have just cited is relevant, not only to the attitude which we hope the representatives of nuclear powers will adopt in their conversations with the Negotiating Committee at United Nations Headquarters, but also to the pace at which our Preparatory Commission should do its work. It should be noted that the representative whom I have quoted—and who is none other than the representative of the United Kingdom, Lord Chalfont, who holds the rank of Minister of State in his government—has spoken not of years, but of months, when referring to the time still available to prevent the spread of nuclear weapons.

The representative of Brazil, who is a Vice-Chairman of our Commission, has correctly stated in the first of his important declarations in the debates of our present session that "the eyes of the world are

[21] United Nations Doc. ENDC/152, 22 Mar. 1965.
[22] United Nations Doc. ENDC/PV.225, 19 Aug. 1965.

on us" and that "it is necessary that we unhesitatingly press onward with our efforts, and that Latin America, with its ever-present tradition of pacificism and of recourse to legal means for the solution of its conflicts, give the world the first example of an agreement for the proscription of the weapons that today endanger the very existence of the human species."

Entirely sharing the ideas of my distinguished colleague, Ambassador Sette Camara, I should like to add that, among the peoples of the world, our own Latin American peoples are the ones who are most closely watching us. Therefore, I trust that when it becomes time to convert into a treaty the draft treaty that we all hope to draw up this coming year, there will be no member state of the Preparatory Commission which will want to take the responsibility of granting the right of veto to any state, be it large or small, nuclear or non-nuclear, continental or extracontinental. Any veto on a matter like the one we are dealing with would be absolutely unacceptable because on this matter depends the very survival of present and future generations of Latin Americans and, in the final analysis, of all mankind.

9 Speech Delivered at the Opening Meeting of the Third Session of the Preparatory Commission for the Denuclearization of Latin America ▪ on 19 April 1966

Almost eight months have passed since we closed the last session of the Preparatory Commission for the Denuclearization of Latin America on 2 September 1965. This is the longest period of time to elapse between our meetings, which began in November 1964 with the work of the Preliminary Meeting. Barely three and a half months later the First Session of our Commission took place, to be followed five months later by the Second Session. But even though we have never delayed so long in resuming our work, neither has the Commission ever had before it such convincing proof of the productive activities of its subsidiary organs as is furnished by the documents that appear on our agenda.

I doubt that there could be anything more encouraging to the accomplishment of the task assigned to us by the Commission in its Resolution 10 (II)—namely, to complete in this session the Preliminary Draft of the Treaty for the Denuclearization of Latin America—than the examination I shall make, brief though it may be, of these documents.

I shall refer first of all to the basic Working Paper COPREDAL/CC/DT/1 submitted to us by the Coordinating Committee. This document, prepared by the Committee "to fulfill the provisions of Resolution 9 (II) and to carry out the functions assigned to the Committee in Resolution 1 (I)" when it was created by the Preparatory Commission, will unquestionably make a valuable contribution to the successful conclusion of the work that we begin today.

47

Inasmuch as the text of the Working Paper is sufficiently explicit in itself, especially if it is studied in the light of the observations contained in its attached commentary, I shall mention only the points that I consider most interesting.

It should be stated that for the first time the Commission has available a document permitting it to understand fully the various questions on which it will have to give an opinion in order to finish its preparation of the Preliminary Draft of the Treaty for the Denuclearization of Latin America. This comprehensive presentation is not the result of an improvised or superficial study. It was painstakingly prepared by the Coordinating Committee, in accordance with the instructions given to it in Resolution 9 (II), on the basis of the preliminary draft articles annexed to this resolution and of observations received from the governments. It is, therefore, a document that is the logical and orderly culmination of the work both of the Preparatory Commission and of its subsidiary organs; a document that has been carefully revised in lengthy discussions of the Coordinating Committee and that has benefited from the objective and eclectic spirit of the members of the Committee.

Thus, for example, the new provisions relative to the control system define specifically the three objectives of this system, which, in synthesis, are to ensure that: the special fissionable materials intended for peaceful purposes are not used for military ends; the treaty is not violated by the introduction of nuclear weapons from abroad; and explosions for peaceful purposes are compatible with the provisions of this treaty.

Additional examples, which could easily be multiplied, are: the detailed explanation of the functions and powers of the principal organs of the permanent Latin American agency to be established; the broadening of the definition of the term "territory" to include not only the territorial sea and air space, but also any other space over which—as in the case of the continental shelf—the state has sovereignty; a new definition of "nuclear weapons," which from a technical point of view appears to be fully adequate for the purposes of a treaty for denuclearization such as the one envisaged by Latin America; the provisions making clear that the so-called "source materials," such as natural uranium and thorium, will not be subject to the Safeguards System of the International Atomic Energy Agency, in order not to impede the use constantly made of such materials for peaceful purposes and also, chiefly, because in Latin America they are unlikely to be applied to military purposes; the careful drafting to firmly establish that the treaty for denuclearization will not stand in the way of nuclear explosions for peaceful purposes; and finally, the provisions that probably cover all the questions referred to in the "final clauses" of a treaty. The foregoing innovations and improvements, incorporated into the Working Paper submitted to us by the Coordinating Committee, make this the most complete and elaborate document that we have considered to date.

The two annexes of the Working Paper, which contain proposals to permit, in due course, formal relations between the Latin American agency—to be known as the Center for the Denuclearization of Latin America[23] and the International Atomic Energy Agency (IAEA) also deserve special mention. The Coordinating Committee made notable progress in these aspects, thanks to the valuable technical aid of the Director-General of the IAEA, Mr. Sigvard Ekelund, and of his designated Observer, Mr. Reinhard Rainer.

The pact between the two agencies, which may be based on one or two basic agreements as required by the circumstances, would enable the Latin American agency to count on the cooperation of the IAEA in effectively operating, with a view to achieving the three objectives already mentioned, the control system established in the treaty. This means that the Safeguards System of the IAEA would be applied so that it not only would ensure that nuclear materials and installations intended for peaceful purposes would not be used to secure military advantages, but also would prevent traffic in nuclear weapons and would supervise such nuclear explosions for peaceful purposes as may become necessary.

The Statute of the IAEA contains provisions of particular relevance in this matter, which leads us to hope that the collaboration of the IAEA will assume the broad outlines I have just sketched. Article III (B) of the Statute stipulates that the Agency, in carrying out its functions, shall:

Conduct its activities in accordance with the purposes and principles of the United Nations to promote peace and international co-operation, and in conformity with policies of the United Nations furthering the establishment of safeguarded world-wide disarmament and in conformity with any international agreements entered into pursuant to such policies.

The basic agreement or agreements that the Latin American agency may conclude, acting on behalf of the contracting parties to the treaty for denuclearization, would incorporate the provisions applicable to the treaty, thereby making it unnecessary for the parties to adopt all the provisions of the Safeguards System or to conclude individual agreements with the IAEA. The basic agreement or agreements would replace a series of individual agreements and would ensure uniformity

---

[23] Name changed to Agency for the Denuclearization of Latin America during the third session in April 1966.

of the obligations undertaken, without excluding the possibility of supplementary agreements between each contracting party and the IAEA to cover the circumstances peculiar to each case.

Another valuable document is the report of the Negotiating Committee (Doc.COPREDAL/CN/1), which was instructed by the Preparatory Commission to endeavor, while the twentieth session of the General Assembly was in progress in New York City, "to expedite to the utmost, through negotiations with authorized representatives of the States concerned" the fulfillment of certain objectives, including action designed to obtain from the nuclear powers a commitment to strictly respect the legal instrument on the denuclearization of Latin America.

An analysis of this report also permits us to draw encouraging conclusions, although not as specific as those we derived from the report of the Coordinating Committee.

The high rank of the diplomats appointed by the nuclear states to represent them at the Committee meetings—present were no less than the three ambassadors who represent their respective governments at the Eighteen-Nation Disarmament Committee—is by itself a clear indication of the importance that these states attach to the Latin American initiative.

Obviously, the representatives of the nuclear states were obliged to inform the Negotiating Committee that their respective governments could not undertake any formal commitments on the Latin American plan for denuclearization until they were acquainted with the complete text of the preliminary draft of the treaty. Nonetheless, if the report of the Negotiating Committee is compared with those of Working Groups A and C, which were submitted to the Preparatory Commission at its last session, it will be seen that the Committee made substantial progress in its discussions with the representatives.

Finally, a third positive element in the work of the Negotiating Committee was its thorough study of the procedural aspect of the matter assigned to it. This study resulted in the draft resolution which appears as Annex 2 in the Committee's report.

The Committee has believed that the adoption of such a draft resolution by the General Assembly of the United Nations, once the stages specified in paragraph 7 of its report are covered, would constitute an adequate procedure which, in addition to simplicity and ease of operation, would offer the advantage of permitting not only the nuclear powers, but all the states of the world, whether or not they are members of the United Nations, to contract the proposed commitment.

At the same time that the Coordinating Committee and the Negotiating Committee have advanced in their work, which I have briefly reviewed, the evolution on an international scale of events related to the non-proliferation of nuclear weapons and to projects for regional denuclearization, such as that of Africa, presents a similarly favorable outlook.

It is our hope that the nuclear states will cooperate to make the Treaty for the Denuclearization of Latin America as effective as possible. In this regard, it should be mentioned that one of the leading nuclear powers, the United States of America, has submitted to the Eighteen-Nation Disarmament Committee a revised text for Article 1 of the draft treaty originally presented on 17 August 1965, which is even stricter than the earlier text in prohibiting any assistance to the spread of nuclear weapons, and which is stated in the following terms:

Each of the nuclear-weapon States party to this treaty undertakes:

1. Not to transfer nuclear weapons into the national control of any non-nuclear-weapon State, or into the control of any association of non-nuclear-weapon States.
2. Not to provide to any non-nuclear-weapon State or association of such States—
   (a) assistance in the manufacture of nuclear weapons, in preparations for such manufacture, or in the testing of nuclear weapons; or
   (b) encouragement or inducement to manufacture or otherwise acquire its own nuclear weapons.
3. Not to take any other action which would cause an increase in the total number of States and associations of States having control of nuclear weapons.
4. Not to take any of the actions prohibited in the preceding paragraphs of this Article directly, or indirectly through third States or associations of States, or through units of the armed forces or military personnel of any State, even if such units or personnel are under the command of a military alliance.[24]

It should be recalled also in this respect that among the documents now under consideration by the Eighteen-Nation Committee is a similar draft, originally presented to the General Assembly of the United Nations on 24 September 1965 by the other of the two great nuclear powers, the Soviet Union. Article 1 of this document, carrying its prohibitions even further than the United States text, is worded as follows:

1. Parties to the Treaty possessing nuclear weapons undertake not to transfer such weapons in any form—directly or indirectly, through third States or groups of States—to the ownership or control of States or groups of States not possessing nuclear weapons and not to accord to such States or groups of States the right to participate in the ownership, control, or use of nuclear weapons.

   The said Parties to the Treaty shall not transfer nuclear weapons, or control over them or over their emplacement and use, to units of the

[24] United Nations Doc. ENDC/152/Add. 1.

51

armed forces or military personnel of States not possessing nuclear weapons, even if such units or personnel are under the command of a military alliance.

2. Parties to the Treaty possessing nuclear weapons undertake not to provide assistance—directly or indirectly, through third States or groups of States—to States not at present possessing nuclear weapons in the manufacture, in preparations for the manufacture, or in the testing of such weapons and not to transmit to them any kind of manufacturing, research, or other information or documentation which can be employed for purposes of the manufacture or use of nuclear weapons.[25]

As I had occasion to state last year, this commitment, which is offered by the nuclear powers on their own initiative in the very first article of their respective draft treaties, is essentially the one we want these powers to contract with regard to Latin America. The only addition, which may be considered implicit in the spirit of the provisions I have cited, would be that the nuclear powers undertake to respect the privileged nuclear-free situation of Latin America and, therefore, to refrain from trying to change it through the introduction of nuclear weapons, even though the latter remain under their control.

Furthermore, the General Assembly of the United Nations has explicitly expressed this idea in adopting on 19 November 1965 Resolution 2028 (XX) entitled "Non-proliferation of nuclear weapons." Herein, it was careful to include among the "general principles" that should be used as a basis for the non-proliferation treaty to be drawn up by the Eighteen-Nation Disarmament Committee, the principle appearing in paragraph 2 (e), which provides as follows: "Nothing in the treaty should adversely affect the right of any group of States to conclude regional treaties in order to ensure the total absence of nuclear weapons in their respective territories." It should be borne in mind that this resolution was approved by 93 affirmative votes, including those of the United States, the United Kingdom, and the Soviet Union, and that it was opposed by none.

The favorable climate for the Latin American aspirations which exists in international discussions on analogous questions is indicated by the message that the President of the Council of Ministers of the Soviet Union addressed to the Eighteen-Nation Disarmament Committee on 1 February of this year. Referring to the draft treaty on non-proliferation presented by his government, he made the following declaration of manifest importance:

In order to facilitate agreement on the conclusion of a treaty, the Soviet Government declares its willingness to include in the draft treaty a clause

25 United Nations Doc. A/5976.

on the prohibition of the use of nuclear weapons against non-nuclear States parties to the treaty which have no nuclear weapons in their territory.[26]

The fact that in the Geneva debates there have still been no concrete offers to the same effect by the other nuclear states should not be interpreted, in my opinion, as a refusal to undertake a similar obligation toward a regional agreement for denuclearization, like that of Latin America. Such a refusal would be incompatible with the affirmative vote cast on 3 December 1965 by all the nuclear powers participating in the work of Geneva. At that time, the General Assembly of the United Nations adopted, by a vote of 105 to 0, Resolution 2033 (XX) entitled "Declaration on the denuclearization of Africa," in which the Assembly expressly calls upon "all States to refrain from the use, or the threat of use, of nuclear weapons on the African continent." To reject for Latin America what has been approved for Africa would be an inconceivable and unacceptable discrimination.

The importance attributed to the Latin American enterprise both by governments and by world public opinion is illustrated in the numerous laudatory references to it in the debates of the last General Assembly of the United Nations and in other international meetings; but I shall quote from only two recently expressed opinions.

In the introduction to his Annual Report presented at the twentieth session of the Assembly, the Secretary-General of the United Nations, U Thant, after praising the efforts and encouraging progress of the Latin American republics, stated:

Success in their endeavors will not only be an achievement of great benefit to the States of Latin America, militarily, politically, economically, and socially; it can, indeed, be of great importance to the world at large. It may well have a catalytic effect on other initiatives for denuclearization, for preventing the further spread of nuclear weapons, and for other measures of disarmament.[27]

The United States Secretary of State Dean Rusk, speaking on 22 November before the Second Extraordinary Inter-American Conference held in Río de Janeiro, declared:

The United States has followed with keen and sympathetic interest the efforts of Latin American countries to work out agreed arrangements for excluding the proliferation, the stationing, or storage of nuclear weapons within the territory of Latin American states. We have noted the encouraging progress toward this end which was made during the current year at discussions in Mexico City. The United States believes the project of a nuclear-free zone in Latin America is constructive statesmanship in the best tradition of the hemis-

[26] United Nations Doc. ENDC/167.
[27] GAOR: 20th Sess., 1965, Suppl. No. 1 A (A/6001/Add. 1) .

53

phere. We welcome the effort and would be glad to see it reach a successful conclusion.[28]

Finally, we must emphasize the compelling urgency of preventing the spread of nuclear weapons—and it should be recalled that denuclearization is the most radical and effective means of banning such proliferation—an urgency that today is axiomatic. Although those of us who attended the debates of the First Committee of the General Assembly of the United Nations witnessed this in the statements of representatives from all over the world, it is not necessary to go to the headquarters of the world Organization. It is enough to read the newspaper, which almost daily publishes declarations by statesmen and public figures—ranging in position from the highest to the most modest—by experts, scholars, or philosophers, all of whom agree that we are very close to the crucial point, beyond which it will be impossible to halt the spread of nuclear weapons. I shall refer here only to some of these declarations, choosing the ones made by the heads of state of the nuclear powers.

The President of the United States of America, in a message to the Eighteen-Nation Disarmament Committee on 27 January 1966, stated: "We have, with all mankind, a common interest in acting now to prevent nuclear spread. . . . We must move . . . quickly while there is yet time."[29]

The Prime Minister of the Union of Soviet Socialist Republics, in another message to the same Committee on 1 February 1966, said: "The Soviet Government insists on the need for the immediate conclusion of an agreement on the non-proliferation of nuclear weapons. Unless an end is put to the proliferation of nuclear weapons throughout the world, the danger of the outbreak of a nuclear war will increase many times over."[30]

The Prime Minister of the United Kingdom, in a speech delivered on 12 March 1966, affirmed: "There is one challenge above all others in this vital year in world affairs. This is the urgent need to stop the spread of nuclear weapons."[31]

To the foregoing quotations dealing with the problem at an international level, I shall add only one more which refers particularly to our regional project. The Mexican Minister of Foreign Affairs, in a speech given on 8 February of this year, used the following words: "We believe that it is of the utmost urgency that the noble enterprise initiated in 1963 by the Latin American republics be successfully con-

[28] Organization of American States, Doc. 87.
[29] United Nations Doc. ENDC/PV.235.
[30] United Nations Doc. ENDC/167.
[31] United Nations Doc. ENDC/PV.250.

cluded. . . . We must . . . exert all our efforts and determination so that 1966 may become the 'Year of the Denuclearization of Latin America.' "

Before ending, I should like to recapitulate a few ideas which I consider fundamental and which are solidly supported by the facts that I have reviewed in the present statement.

The Preparatory Commission for the Denuclearization of Latin America reaches this decisive stage of its work in exceptionally favorable conditions. Now it must fulfill the task which it imposed on itself eight months ago; that is, to finish preparation of the Preliminary Draft of the Treaty for the Denuclearization of Latin America.

This task, which perhaps would have been impossibly difficult if an attempt had been made to carry it out hastily and superficially, today appears to be relatively easy, thanks to the fund of knowledge and experience gathered during two years of methodical and constant work, on a scale that can be appreciated in the number of documents now available to the Preparatory Commission.

The widespread and growing preoccupation at international meetings with the grave dangers inherent in the proliferation of nuclear weapons is one more factor which, although accessory, is equally favorable to the work of this Commission.

It should be borne in mind, furthermore, that the Commission is called upon to finish in its Third Session not the Treaty for Denuclearization, but only a preliminary draft of such a treaty. Nevertheless, this preliminary draft, which itself may still be subject to changes, is at this stage an indispensable element in the normal progress of the work toward the denuclearization of Latin America. It is indispensable so that we can request of the nuclear states the formal declaration which we expect from them and which the Negotiating Committee discussed with their representatives; it is indispensable so that those states which have, *de jure* or *de facto*, international responsibility for territories situated in the Western Hemisphere—whose governments are represented on our Commission by observers—can take a decision, which we hope will be positive, with regard to the inclusion of such territories in the treaty; it is indispensable so that formal negotiations may be entered into with the IAEA for the collaboration defined in the two drafts of basic agreement annexed to the Working Paper prepared by the Coordinating Committee; it is indispensable so that, above all, the competent organs of the governments of the member states of the Preparatory Commission can be consulted on a complete text of the document which, in due course, will have to be submitted to a conference of plenipotentiaries in order to become the Treaty for the Denuclearization of Latin America, the treaty anxiously awaited by our peoples and whose catalytic effect is bound to have incalculably beneficial repercussions on world negotiations for disarmament.

The President of Mexico, Gustava Díaz Ordaz, says in the message which he has addressed to us today that "it may be stated without exaggeration that the entire world will follow with close attention" our discussions and that "The Commission's Third Session, which begins today, will go down in history if, as I am sure we all hope, it can successfully conclude preparation of the Preliminary Draft of the Treaty for the Denuclearization of Latin America, as the Commission itself recommended unanimously last year."

Our responsibility is greater than ever because the task on the agenda of this Commission cannot be postponed; because it is of transcendental significance not only for our peoples, but for all mankind; and even because it becomes daily more feasible, especially in the light of the many pitfalls that we have fortunately skirted.

As chairman of the Commission I have been the frequent witness of what our combined efforts can accomplish and I am confident that we shall not fail the hopes of Latin America and of the world. I am also confident that when it comes time to close this session, we shall be able to present to mankind the first preliminary draft, internationally approved, of a treaty for denuclearization, in this case designed to perpetuate the nuclear-free situation enjoyed by Latin America.

10 Speech Delivered at the Closing Meeting of the Third Session of the Preparatory Commission for the Denuclearization of Latin America ▪ on 4 May 1966

As the third session of our Commission draws to a close, I shall, as has been my custom, attempt to assess the results of our work. I shall begin by stating that, contrary to the impression that a casual observer might have gathered from the general debate, I am convinced that the session which is ending has been the most fruitful and positive of the four sessions held in Mexico City from November 1964 to date.

In my opinion, no other international meeting would have been more appropriate than the present one to inaugurate this conference room located on the Plaza of the Three Cultures. Here, Latin America has once again shown its maturity and its ability to appraise correctly the authentic aspirations of its peoples. Our America, in which the indigenous cultures are intermingled with the Latin culture of the Renaissance, lives not in the past but in the midst of the twentieth century, and it clearly recognizes the terrible dangers as well as the advantages of the so-called nuclear era.

A few moments ago I said that it would be a mistake to draw hasty conclusions from the apparent differences of opinion on some aspects of the general debate. Although such differences have existed and still exist, this debate has at the same time highlighted our absolute unanimity of purpose.

Allow me to illustrate this by quoting from some of the speeches, in the order in which they were presented.

The representative of Venezuela stated: "It should be clearly understood that the result of these discussions is that the countries participating in this meeting definitively reject the installation or proliferation of nuclear weapons and are firmly resolved to keep the region and its peoples free from the threat of nuclear war."

The representative of Brazil said:

What we fear above all is that the fifteen or twenty countries which sooner or later will be able to manufacture nuclear weapons, if measures are not taken to halt their advance toward atomic might, may be in a position to decide arbitrarily on the use of such weapons. What we want to avoid above all is the catastrophe that could be the aftermath of the explosion of the first atomic bomb. In modern power politics, it is impossible to predict the rate of "escalation" that would follow the use of the first nuclear weapon, which could set off a conflict capable of destruction on a scale never dreamed of by man.

The representative of Argentina, after expressing his pleasure in collaborating "in an effort of momentous political and human implications, inspired in the best ideals of Latin American thought," added that his delegation "considers that the atmosphere of a denuclearized zone can eliminate tensions among the states that compose it and can help to maintain international peace and security in the area in question."

The representative of Chile said: "The third session to convene in this city, which has become the symbolic center of a common will, again shows the world the sincerity of a bold and selfless aim: the renunciation of the exercise of its sovereign rights by each one of our countries, in the interest of the peaceful development of the international community."

"The Latin American peoples," declared the representative of Ecuador, "want to live in peace, free from the threat of lethal radiation, free from the fear that resources which should be invested in economic improvement, social welfare, and the promotion of greater justice may be used to satisfy the vanity or the madness of those who would like to have an illusory atomic power in the future."

"At the same time that we repeat our belief in the fundamental value of the development of nuclear energy for peaceful purposes, we again affirm the solidarity of Uruguay," said the representative of this country, "with this magnificent effort designed to exclude Latin America from the field of atomic warfare."

"Our country," stated the representative of Colombia, "is prepared to continue supporting any measure aimed at converting the prodigious atomic and nuclear discoveries into weapons for peace, which would improve rather than ravage the human race."

"The delegation of Guatemala," announced its representative, "is glad to collaborate with this third session of the Preparatory Commission, just as it has done in the past, for the purpose of achieving a legal instrument that will satisfy our countries and that will banish from Latin American territories the possibility of destruction inherent in the use of nuclear weapons and their proliferation."

In addition to having brought out the fact that we share a single objective—to make permanent the total absence of nuclear weapons from Latin American territories—the third session of the Commission can be credited with having unanimously approved, and the importance of this can hardly be exaggerated, in the document entitled "Proposals for the Preparation of the Treaty for the Denuclearization of Latin America" numerous texts of a substantive nature which will eventually be included in this treaty and will probably make up about 90 per cent of its contents. Although alternative texts for the remaining 10 per cent will have to be submitted to the governments, they will serve to define the questions on which the member states should concentrate their efforts in order to eliminate differences of opinion and obtain the consensus that we all desire.

On an earlier occasion similar to the present, I remarked that, when future generations of Latin America look for the origin of the noble enterprise that banished the threat of nuclear warfare from their homeland, they will regard with respect three documents: the Joint Declaration of 29 April 1963; Resolution 1911 (XVIII) of the United Nations; and Resolution II of the Preliminary Meeting on the Denuclearization of Latin America, which created the Preparatory Commission.

Today I should like to add that, when these same generations study the documents that marked the beginning of the completion of this enterprise, they will come across four other equally significant documents: the Observations of the Mexican Government on the Preliminary Draft of the Multilateral Treaty for the Denuclearization of Latin America, in which for the first time, on 15 January 1966, the complete text of a possible preliminary draft was formulated; the Working Paper submitted by the Coordinating Committee to this Commission on 14 March of this year, which was also drawn up in the form of a preliminary draft of the treaty; the draft of the Treaty for the Denuclearization of Latin America, which was presented by the delegation of Brazil on 20 April and co-sponsored a few days later by the delegation of Colombia; and finally, the Proposals for the Preparation of the Treaty for the Denuclearization of Latin America, which we unanimously approved yesterday.

The Dumbarton Oaks Proposals undoubtedly have a place of honor in the history of the United Nations as the immediate predecessor of the San Francisco Charter. Our proposals, which may one day be called the Tlatelolco Proposals, will likewise occupy (perhaps more rightfully, inasmuch as the former proposals constituted only the embryo of what was to be the Charter of the world organization, whereas ours may very well represent almost the entirety of the future Treaty) a place of special significance in the annals of the denuclearization of Latin America.

I am convinced that the ideas expressed by the representatives who participated in the general debate and whom I cited at the beginning of this talk, faithfully reflect the sentiments and aspirations of all of us and of all our peoples and governments. I also believe in the saying that where there's a will there's a way, which makes me sure that in the not too distant future we can realize the objective that we strive for.

We have advanced perhaps slowly, but surely, in our work. We can also feel proud that there have been no setbacks. With the result of its efforts of the last two weeks, the Preparatory Commission has shown once again that the decision of the peoples of Latin America to use the imponderable force of the atom—as the President of Mexico said a few days ago—"for life, not for death," is an irrevocable one.

The Commission always has tried to act with prudence and caution, which it would be a mistake to interpret as irresponsibility and indecision. Our work, gaining in vigor and drive with every meeting, is a dynamic process that will inevitably lead to the signing and entry into force of the Treaty for the Denuclearization of Latin America. It is this treaty which present generations of our countries demand and which future generations would never forgive us for failing to achieve.

11 Speech Delivered at the Only Meeting of the First Part of the Fourth Session of the Preparatory Commission for the Denuclearization of Latin America ■ on 30 August 1966

Before closing the first part of the fourth session of the Preparatory Commission, which we inaugurated today in accordance with Resolution 16 (III) of the Commission itself, I should like to say a few words about the past, present, and future of our work. I shall limit my references to the past to a brief review of the most important recent developments in our work since 4 May of this year, when we closed the third session.

I shall first mention that three member states, Chile, Uruguay, and Venezuela, have submitted observations on the proposals endorsed by Resolution 14 (III). Everyone is familiar with the documents, circulated by the Secretariat of the Commission, in which these observations are reproduced. I do not propose to analyze them; the Commission will have the time to do so in due course. I shall make only two general remarks. The first is that, whatever views the representatives may have on these observations, I am sure we all agree that they reflect the constructive spirit which has undoubtedly inspired their authors. The second is that I believe it would be a great mistake to attribute the relatively small number of observations received to any lack of interest on the part of the member states. I am quite certain that in some cases the lack of time, caused by circumstances beyond control has prevented some states from presenting their observations. In others, the chief reason has been that the member states have generally considered the draft of the Treaty for the Denuclearization of Latin America embodied in the proposals to be, in the words of the Uruguayan government, "satisfactory," and they are reserving their suggestions for the sessions when the Commission, either directly or through working groups, devotes itself to the task of giving final form to the treaty.

In respect of the non-member states, with whom the Negotiating Committee began discussion in 1965, it should be pointed out that of the five notes received from them, four—including those of three nuclear states—are favorable.

The government of the Netherlands has repeated its agreement, under provisions of the draft treaty, "to contract the same obligations with regard to Surinam and the Netherlands Antilles that the Latin American countries contract with regard to the denuclearization of Latin America."

The French government, after reaffirming its sympathy with the efforts of the Latin American countries, has made known categorically its "intention of not taking any action with regard to the Latin American states that would encourage in their territories the development of nuclear activities of a military nature," and goes on to recall that, as it had previously informed the Commission, "concerning our departments in America . . . France has no intention of carrying out nuclear experiments in them and, in particular, that the activities of the Space Center of Guiana relate only to tests of spacial rockets and the launching of satellites."

The government of the United Kingdom, referring to Article 20 of the proposals, which deals with the question of the "signature and accession" to the future treaty, has stated that "Her Majesty's Government have consulted the Administrations of all British dependent territories within the proposed area indicated in this Article" and that "none of these has any objection to their inclusion in a Treaty provided the provisions are otherwise acceptable."

With regard to Article 23, which sets forth the provisions whereby the treaty "shall enter into force," the same government, after recalling its principle that nuclear-free zones should include "all militarily significant states, and preferably all states," defines its position on this question in the following terms:

Her Majesty's Government . . . would not exclude the possibility of giving support to a restricted zone which excluded some states, even militarily significant ones, if such a restricted zone would have a reasonable prospect of existing as a viable entity and particularly if it appeared likely to form a reasonable foundation on which a comprehensive zone could be built.

The government of the United States of America begins its reply with a very encouraging statement which reads as follows:

The United States has followed with interest the efforts to achieve a nuclear-free zone in Latin America, and we welcome the effort and would be glad to see it reach a successful conclusion. Such success would constitute an excellent example of Latin American leadership and would strengthen world peace by helping to prevent the spread of nuclear weapons while maintaining hemispheric security.

The United States reply continues with specific observations, which the Commission will comment on in due course. I should like to point out only that, when the competent organ, which probably will be the General Conference, enters into "relations with other international organizations" as provided for in Article 14, the special character of the Agency for the Denuclearization of Latin America must be taken into account. Although this agency will be basically Latin American, its membership will include extra-continental states, which will undertake only to contract obligations with regard to territories situated in the western hemisphere south of latitude 30° North. In this connection, the observation of the British government should be cited:

Her Majesty's Government are not a member of the Organization of American States and would be unable to accept obligations in respect of the inter-American system even if they became full contracting parties to a Treaty with equal status with all other contracting parties.

The failure of the Union of Soviet Socialist Republics to reply to the Commission, despite the lapse of time since Resolution 14 (III) was adopted and the action taken by the Coordinating Committee, should not, in my view, be interpreted as a sign of a negative attitude on the denuclearization of Latin America. This delay is more likely due to reasons of another nature which it is not within my competence to analyze on this occasion.

My conviction is based on the "praise of the Commission's aims and of its work," as expressed by the representatives of all the nuclear powers participating in the Eighteen-Nation Disarmament Committee which was noted by the Coordinating Committee in its resolution of 15 August. As an example, allow me to recall the statement of the representative of the Soviet Union in the meeting of the Eighteen-Nation Disarmament Committee held on 2 August of this year. After referring to the existing projects for the creation of denuclearized zones, among which he specifically mentioned that of Latin America, he said:

The Soviet Union is a resolute advocate of the establishment of denuclearized zones in various parts of the world, since the accomplishment of this measure would open the way to an effective restriction of the sphere of location and use of nuclear weapons and consequently to a diminution of the threat of nuclear war and to a limitation of the arms race.[32]

Statements as forceful as those I have just quoted and several others that have been recorded in previous meetings of our Commission have convinced me that long before the opening of the fourth session the Secretariat of the Commission will be able to distribute to member states the missing reply and that it will be essentially positive. A negative reply would signify an inconceivable conflict between deeds and words, between statements and conduct.

Having just referred to the Eighteen-Nation Disarmament Committee, I should like to mention here some of the progress it made in its last session, ending on 25 August, which is intimately linked to our enterprise. As we know, the General Assembly of the United Nations adopted at its twentieth session Resolution 2028, which stated that the non-proliferation treaty under preparation by the Committee should include the following principle: "Nothing in the treaty should adversely affect the right of any group of States to conclude regional treaties in order to ensure the total absence of nuclear weapons in their respective territories."

In its most recent discussions, the Committee dealt with this question, and the following paragraph relative to the principle I have just cited was inserted into the memorandum that was approved unanimously by the non-aligned countries on 19 August:

The eight delegations find [the] principle . . . of great interest to countries in some regions where it is possible to reach agreement on a treaty on denuclearization, which is in itself a measure of non-proliferation. They trust that there will be no difficulty in embodying a provision corresponding to this principle in the text of a treaty on non-proliferation.[33]

In addition to the eight delegations of the non-aligned countries, the representatives of four other countries, two from the western bloc and two from the eastern bloc, previously had made analogous declarations. Therefore, to date, twelve of the seventeen countries participating in the work of the Eighteen-Nation Disarmament Committee, or two-thirds of the total membership, favor adoption of an article the chief purpose of which is to keep the proposed non-proliferation treaty from adversely affecting the conclusion of treaties like the one for the denuclearization of Latin America.

If we turn from the immediate past to the present, I believe that we shall find similar reasons for encouragement. During the month that is about to end, a substantial number of member states requested postponement of the fourth session, while an equally sizable group pre-

[32] United Nations Doc. ENDC/PV.278.
[33] United Nations Doc. ENDC/178.

ferred that the date originally set by the Commission be maintained. Nevertheless, thanks to frank and sincere exchanges of points of view, through which it was possible to assess the needs of the one group and to dispel the preoccupations of the other, these legitimate differences of opinion have been easily erased. The result has been the text of the resolution that today we unanimously adopted.

This procedure of consultation, of mutual understanding and conciliation ending in consensus, is a good omen for the future of our work, to which I shall refer briefly. But first I wish to extend a cordial welcome to the two new observers from Belgium and Finland, who attend the meetings of the Commission for the first time and who, added to the already accredited observers, raise the total to eighteen.

I believe that an analysis of the text of Resolution 19 (IV) will furnish valuable elements for appraising the future of our work. We have all agreed to postpone until 31 January 1967 the debates of the session inaugurated today, not out of apathy or indifference or obstructionism, but as the resolution states, "to expedite the successful conclusion of the work of the Commission" and in order to "contribute to the creation of the most favorable conditions for the preparation of the Treaty for the Denuclearization of Latin America," noting at the same time "the compelling urgency of completing the task" that has been entrusted to the Commission "for the good of the peoples of Latin America and of all mankind." Therefore, the Commission decided "to urge the governments of the member states to give priority during this interval, to the study of the points of the Draft Treaty for the Denuclearization of Latin America that are still pending."

I am convinced that faithful fulfillment of the commitment implied by the provisions of the resolution which was approved today can be decisive in enabling the Commission to conclude successfully the preparation of the Treaty for the Denuclearization of Latin America in the second part of its fourth session. In this connection, I should like to mention observations received from two governments that deserve serious consideration.

In the first, the government of Chile used the following words:

It does not appear reasonable that the states which, after taking into account all the risks and circumstances, wish to associate themselves with an objective as noble and significant as that expressed by the Treaty for the Denuclearization of Latin America, should have their aims and aspirations frustrated by a series of requirements in the same treaty that either make impossible or delay indefinitely its entry into force.

The second was submitted by the government of the Netherlands:

The government of the Kingdom of the Netherlands would regret that any country, whether one of the Latin American countries or one of the nuclear powers, should be afforded the opportunity of preventing the proposed denuclearization by refusing to cooperate with the treaty in question.

Before ending, I should like to emphasize the significance of the task that has been assigned to us by recalling paragraphs taken, respectively, from the messages delivered last April to the Commission by the President of Mexico, Gustavo Díaz Ordaz, and by the Secretary-General of the United Nations, U Thant. At that time, the Mexican head of state said: "Latin America, faithful to its tradition of peace and universal cooperation, today has the opportunity of making an invaluable contribution to mankind by giving it the first example of an international agreement for denuclearization."

The highest official of the world organization declared: "Success in your enterprise will be not only an achievement of great benefit to the Latin American States, but it can, indeed, be of great importance to the world at large." [34]

I close this first part of the fourth session of the Preparatory Commission for the Denuclearization of Latin America firmly convinced that the recess will by no means be a recession, in spite of the similarity of the two words. All to the contrary. If, as is our duty, we use to advantage the five intervening months before we resume our work, we shall, I am sure, be surprised to find that our seemingly difficult task has become easy and feasible. We shall have thus confirmed once more that our Commission is worthy of the confidence placed in it by all the peoples of Latin America.

[34] Unofficial translation.

Part Two

INTERNATIONAL

DOCUMENTS

12 Joint Declaration of 29 April 1963 on the Denuclearization of Latin America[1]

The Presidents of the Republics of Bolivia, Brazil, Chile, Ecuador and Mexico,

Deeply concerned about the present turn of events in the international situation, which is conducive to the spread of nuclear weapons,

Considering that, in virtue of their unchanging peace-loving tradition, the Latin American States should unite their efforts in order to turn Latin America into a denuclearized zone, thus helping to reduce the dangers that threaten world peace,

Wishing to preserve their countries from the tragic consequences attendant upon a nuclear war, and

Spurred by the hope that the conclusion of a Latin American regional agreement will contribute to the adoption of a contractual instrument of world-wide application,

In the name of their peoples and Governments have agreed as follows:

1. To announce forthwith that their Governments are prepared to sign a multilateral Latin American agreement whereby their countries would undertake not to manufacture, receive, store or test nuclear weapons or nuclear launching devices;

2. To bring this Declaration to the attention of the Heads of State of the other Latin American Republics, expressing the hope that their Governments will accede to it through such procedure as they consider appropriate;

[1] Reproduced in GAOR: 18th Sess., 1963, Annexes, Agenda item 74 (Doc. A/5415/-Rev. 1).

69

3. To co-operate with one another and with such other Latin American Republics as accede to this Declaration, in order that Latin America may be recognized as a denuclearized zone as soon as possible.

13 Resolution 1911 (XVIII) on the Denuclearization of Latin America ▪ Approved by the General Assembly of the United Nations ▪ on 27 November 1963

The General Assembly,

Bearing in mind the vital necessity of sparing present and future generations the scourge of a nuclear war,

Recalling its resolutions 1380 (XIV) of 20 November 1959, 1576 (XV) of 20 December 1960 and 1965 (XVI) of 4 December 1961, in which it recognized the danger that an increase in the number of States possessing nuclear weapons would involve, since such an increase would necessarily result in an intensification of the arms race and an aggravation of the difficulty of maintaining world peace, thus rendering more difficult the attainment of a general disarmament agreement,

Observing that in its resolution 1664 (XVI) of 4 December 1961 it stated explicitly that the countries not possessing nuclear weapons had a grave interest and an important part to fulfil in the preparation and implementation of measures that could halt further nuclear weapon tests and prevent the further spread of nuclear weapons,

Considering that the recent conclusion of the Treaty banning nuclear weapon tests in the atmosphere, in outer space and under water, signed on 5 August 1963, has created a favourable atmosphere for parallel progress towards the prevention of the further spread of nuclear weapons, a problem which, as indicated in General Assembly resolutions 1649 (XVI) of 8 November 1961 and 1762 (XVII) of 6

November 1962, is closely connected with that of the banning of nuclear weapon tests,

Considering that the Heads of State of five Latin American Republics issued, on 29 April 1963, a declaration on the denuclearization of Latin America in which, in the name of their peoples and Governments, they announced that they are prepared to sign a multilateral Latin American agreement whereby their countries would undertake not to manufacture, receive, store or test nuclear weapons or nuclear launching devices,

Recognizing the need to preserve, in Latin America, conditions which will prevent the countries of the region from becoming involved in a dangerous and ruinous nuclear arms race,

1. *Notes with satisfaction* the initiative for the denuclearization of Latin America taken in the joint declaration of 29 April 1963;
2. *Expresses the hope* that the States of Latin America will initiate studies, as they deem appropriate, in the light of the principles of the Charter of the United Nations and of regional agreements and by the means and through the channels which they deem suitable, concerning the measures that should be agreed upon with a view to achieving the aims of the said declaration;
3. *Trusts* that at the appropriate moment, after a satisfactory agreement has been reached, all States, particularly the nuclear Powers, will lend their full co-operation for the effective realization of the peaceful aims inspiring the present resolution;
4. *Requests* the Secretary-General to extend to the States of Latin America, at their request, such technical facilities as they may require in order to achieve the aims set forth in the present resolution.

1265th plenary meeting, 27 November 1963.

14 Final Act of the Preliminary Meeting on the Denuclearization of Latin America ▪ held in Mexico City ▪ from 23 to 27 November 1964[2]

The Preliminary Meeting on the Denuclearization of Latin America was held at Mexico City from 23 to 27 November 1964, in accordance with the provisions of paragraph 2 of resolution 1911 (XVIII) of the United Nations General Assembly and in response to the invitation extended by the Government of Mexico.

The seventeen Latin American Republics which, together with the membership of their respective delegations, are listed below, and which all voted in favour of the above-mentioned resolution at the eighteenth session of the General Assembly, were represented at the Meeting as follows:

ARGENTINA: *Representative:* Ambassador Silvano Santander; *Alternate representative:* Mr. Fidel González Paz

BOLIVIA: *Representative:* Ambassador Roberto Querejazu Calvo

BRAZIL: *Representative:* Ambassador José Sette Camara; *Alternate representative:* Mr. Octavio Luiz de Berenguer César; *Advisor:* Mr. Marcos Castrioto de Azambuja

CHILE: *Representative:* Ambassador Alberto Sepúlveda Contreras; *Alternate representative:* Mr. Aurelio Fernández García-Huidobro

2 Reproduced in United Nations Doc. A/5824, 3 Dec. 1964.

73

COLOMBIA: *Representative:* Mr. Carlos Escallón Villa

COSTA RICA: *Representative:* Ambassador Fernando Barrenechea C.

DOMINICAN REPUBLIC: *Representative:* Ambassador José Antonio Fernández Caminero

ECUADOR: *Representative:* Ambassador Leopoldo Benites Vinueza

EL SALVADOR: *Representative:* Ambassador Rafael Eguizábal Tobías

HAITI: *Representative:* Ambassador Julio Jean Pierre-Audain

HONDURAS: *Representative:* Ambassador Federico Poujol; *Alternate representatives:* Mrs. Clotilde Aguilar de Colmant; Mr. Manuel Camero

MEXICO: *Representative:* Ambassador Alfonso García Robles; *Alternate representative:* Ambassador Ismael Moreno Pino; *Advisors:* Mr. Jesús Cabrera Muñoz-Ledo; Mr. Ángel López Padilla; Dr. Carlos Graef Fernández

NICARAGUA: *Representative:* Ambassador Alejandro Argüello Montiel

PANAMA: *Representative:* Mr. José B. Calvo

PARAGUAY: *Representative:* Ambassador J. Natalicio González; *Alternate representative:* Mr. Alberto Preda Llamosas

PERU: *Representative:* Ambassador Álvaro Rey de Castro

URUGUAY: *Observer:* Mr. Aníbal Abadie-Aicardi

The Meeting's deliberations were conducted in accordance with the rules of procedure of the United Nations General Assembly.

The Meeting's agenda consisted of the two following items:

1. Measures that should be agreed upon with a view to achieving the purposes of the denuclearization of Latin America as set forth in the Declaration of 29 April 1963 and reiterated in resolution 1911 (XVIII) of the United Nations General Assembly.

2. Preliminary examination of the principal considerations involved in the conclusion of a contractual instrument on the denuclearization of Latin America.

At the opening meeting, the following officers were appointed by acclamation:

Chairman: Ambassador Alfonso García Robles, Representative of Mexico

Vice-Chairmen: Ambassador José Sette Camara, Representative of Brazil; Ambassador Rafael Eguizábal Tobías, Representative of El Salvador

Ambassador Carlos Peón del Valle served as General Secretary of the Meeting, to which office he had been appointed earlier by the Government of Mexico.

Mr. Donaciano González served as Deputy Secretary and Mr. Antonio González de León, Mr. Sergio González Gálvez and Mr. José Luis Vallarta as Assistant Secretaries.

As a result of its discussions, the Preliminary Meeting unanimously adopted the following resolutions:

I/*Reaffirmation of the proposed denuclearization of Latin America*

The Preliminary Meeting on the Denuclearization of Latin America,
Considering

That the growing spread of nuclear weapons tends to increase international tension and the risk of world war,

That for the purposes of the Meeting "denuclearization" shall mean the absence of nuclear weapons and nuclear launching devices,

That the peaceful use of nuclear energy is very important for economic and scientific development,

Decides

1. To reaffirm the aims set forth in the joint Declaration of 29 April 1963 and ratified in resolution 1911 (XVIII) of the United Nations General Assembly on the denuclearization of Latin America;

2. To stress the advisability of promoting international co-operation for the peaceful use of nuclear energy, especially for the benefit of the developing countries.

II/*Establishment of a Preparatory Commission for the Denuclearization of Latin America*

The Preliminary Meeting on the Denuclearization of Latin America
Decides

1. To establish a Preparatory Commission for the Denuclearization of Latin America, which shall have its headquarters in Mexico and be composed of the seventeen Latin American Republics which have participated in the Meeting and those which subsequently accede to this resolution.

   The Commission shall elect its Chairman and the other officers which it deems appropriate, and shall adopt its own rules of procedure;

2. To instruct the Preparatory Commission to prepare a preliminary draft of a multilateral treaty for the denuclearization of Latin America and, to this end, to undertake the preparatory studies and measures which it considers appropriate.

The Commission shall constitute from its membership the working groups which it deems necessary and which shall perform their functions either at the headquarters of the Commission or elsewhere, as appropriate, and a committee to co-ordinate their work, to be called the "Co-ordinating Committee".

At the beginning of its work, the Commission shall consider the ideas expressed during the discussions at the Preliminary Meeting and reported in its records.

In fulfilling its mandate, the Commission shall act in the light of the principles of the Charter of the United Nations and of regional agreements;

3. To recommend that the Preparatory Commission should give priority in its work to the following matters:

(a) the definition of the geographical boundaries of the area to which the treaty should apply;

(b) the methods of verification, inspection and control that should be adopted to ensure the faithful fulfilment of the obligations contracted under the treaty;

(c) action designed to secure the collaboration in the Commission's work of the Latin American Republics that were not represented at the Preliminary Meeting;

(d) action designed to ensure that the extra-continental or continental States which, in addition to the Latin American Republics, exercise *de jure* or *de facto* international responsibility for territories situated within the boundaries of the geographical area to which the treaty applies, agree to contract the same obligations with regard to those territories as the above-mentioned Republics contract with regard to their own;

(e) action designed to obtain from the nuclear Powers a commitment to the effect that they will strictly respect the legal instrument on the denuclearization of Latin America as regards all its aspects and consequences;

4. To fix Monday, 15 March 1965, as the date of the first meeting of the Preparatory Commission in Mexico City;

5. To request the Governments of the seventeen Latin American Republics which have participated in the Preliminary Meeting to designate their respective representatives to the Preparatory Commission sufficiently in advance of the date specified in the preceding paragraph;

6. To request the Government of Mexico to appoint the General Secretary of the Preparatory Commission and to provide suitable premises and the necessary staff for the secretariat of the Commission.

III/*Tribute to President Adolfo López Mateos*

The Preliminary Meeting on the Denuclearization of Latin America,
Considering

That His Excellency don Adolfo López Mateos, President of the United Mexican States, in carrying out an international policy of peace aimed at the fulfilment of the highest human ideals, has been a dynamic and enthusiastic champion of the proposals for the denuclearization of Latin America,

That the personal initiative displayed in his letter of 21 March 1963 led to the joint Declaration of 29 April of that year, which is one of the basic documents setting forth the ideal of freeing Latin America from the scourge of nuclear war,

That, through his Government's efforts, this Preliminary Meeting on the Denuclearization of Latin America has been held in an atmosphere of cordiality, freedom and true Americanism,

Decides to place on record its tribute to the eminent American citizen, His Excellency don Adolfo López Mateos, President of the United Mexican States.

IV/*Vote of thanks*

The Preliminary Meeting on the Denuclearization of Latin America,
Considering

The exceptional efficiency and flawless organization with which the relevant services of the Mexican Government have ensured the progress of its work and the full achievement of its objectives,

Decides to address a vote of thanks to the said Government, with a special word of praise for Ambassadors Alfonso García Robles and Carlos Peón del Valle and their colleagues for their invaluable services.

V/*Transmission of the Final Act to the International Atomic Energy Agency and the Inter-American Nuclear Energy Commission*

The Preliminary Meeting on the Denuclearization of Latin America
Decides to request the General Secretary of the Meeting to transmit the text of this Final Act to the Director General of the International Atomic Energy Agency and to the Executive Secretary of the Inter-American Nuclear Energy Commission, in connexion with resolution I, paragraph 2.

VI/*Transmission of the Final Act to the United Nations*

The Preliminary Meeting on the Denuclearization of Latin America
Decides to ask the Chairman of the Meeting to transmit to the Secre-

tary-General of the United Nations the text of this Final Act, with the request that he should have it distributed as a General Assembly document for the information of Members of the United Nations in connexion with resolution 1911 (XVIII), paragraph 2.

This Final Act was unanimously adopted by the Preliminary Meeting on the Denuclearization of Latin America at its closing meeting on Friday, 27 November 1964, the first anniversary of the adoption of resolution 1911 (XVIII).

15 Final Act of the First Session of the Preparatory Commission for the Denuclearization of Latin America ▪ held in Mexico City ▪ from 15 to 22 March 1965[3]

The first session of the Preparatory Commission for the Denuclearization of Latin America was held at Mexico City from 15 to 22 March 1965, in accordance with the provisions of paragraph 4 of resolution II of the Preliminary Meeting on the Denuclearization of Latin America and the notice given by the General Secretary on 26 February 1965.

The Latin American Republics which, together with the membership of their respective delegations, are listed below were represented at the session:

ARGENTINA: *Representative:* Ambassador Silvano Santander; *Alternate representative:* Mr. Samuel Daien

BOLIVIA: *Alternate representative:* Mr. Walter Arce Pacheco

BRAZIL: *Representative:* Ambassador José Sette Camara; *Alternate representative:* Mr. Octavio Luiz de Berenguer César; *Adviser:* Mr. Marcos Castrioto de Azambuja

CHILE: *Representative:* Ambassador Horacio Suárez Herreros; *Alternate representative:* Mr. Enrique Cobo del Campo

COLOMBIA: *Representative:* Mr. Carlos Escallón Villa; *Alternate representative:* Mr. Jorge Quintero y Quintero

[3] Reproduced in United Nations Doc. A/5912, 15 Apr. 1965.

COSTA RICA: *Representative:* Ambassador Fernando Barrenechea; *Alternate representative:* Mr. Carlos A. Moreno

DOMINICAN REPUBLIC: *Representative:* Ambassador José Antonio Fernández Caminero; *Alternate representative:* Mr. Tulio Enrique Martí Brenes

ECUADOR: *Representative:* Ambassador Fernando Chávez

EL SALVADOR: *Representative:* Ambassador Rafael Eguizábal Tobías

HAITI: *Representative:* Ambassador Julio Jean Pierre-Audain

HONDURAS: *Representative:* Ambassador Federico E. Poujol; *Alternate representative:* Mr. Manuel Gamero

MEXICO: *Representative:* Ambassador Alfonso García Robles; *Alternate representative:* Ambassador Ismael Moreno Pino; *Advisers:* Mr. Jesús Cabrera Muñoz-Ledo, Mr. Edmundo Castro Villarreal, Mr. Agustín Muñoz de Cote, Mr. Carlos Graef Fernández

NICARAGUA: *Representative:* Ambassador Alejandro Argüello Montiel; *Alternate representative:* Mr. Santos Vanegas Gutiérrez

PANAMA: *Representative:* Ambassador José B. Cárdenas; *Alternate representative:* Mr. José B. Calvo

PARAGUAY: *Representative:* Ambassador J. Natalicio González

PERU: *Representative:* Ambassador Álvaro Rey de Castro; *Adviser:* Mr. Noé Hernán Ramírez Lituma

URUGUAY: *Representative:* Enrique Rodríguez Fabregat; *Alternate representative:* Mr. Aníbal Abadie-Aicardi; *Adviser:* Mr. Alfredo Giró

VENEZUELA: *Representative:* Ambassador Rolando Salcedo Delima

The Government of Guatemala accredited Mr. Francisco Linares Aranda, its Ambassador to Mexico, as observer.

The Government of the Netherlands accredited Mr. L.A.M. Lichtveld as observer.

The Government of Yugoslavia accredited Mr. Dalibor Soldatić, its Ambassador to Mexico, as observer.

The deliberations of the Preparatory Commission were centred upon the following item which appeared in its agenda:

Preparation of the preliminary draft of a multilateral treaty for the denuclearization of Latin America and, to that end, execution of the preparatory measures and studies referred to in resolution II of the Preliminary Meeting on the Denuclearization of Latin America.

At its first meeting, the Preparatory Commission elected the following officers by acclamation:

Chairman: Ambassador Alfonso García Robles, Representative of Mexico.

Vice-Chairmen: Ambassador José Sette Camara, Representative of Brazil, and Ambassdor Rafael Eguizábal Tobías, Representative of El Salvador.

Ambassador Carlos Peón del Valle, having been appointed by the Government of Mexico in accordance with paragraph 6 of resolution II of the Preliminary Meeting on the Denuclearization of Latin America, served as General Secretary of the Preparatory Commission.

Mr. Carlos González Parrodi served as Deputy Secretary and Mr. Antonio González de León, Mr. Sergio González Gálvez and Mr. José Luis Vallarta as Assistant Secretaries.

During its discussion at the first and second meetings, on 15 and 16 March 1965, the Preparatory Commission took note of the communications addressed to the General Secretary by the diplomatic missions of Guatemala and the Netherlands accredited to Mexico concerning the attendance of its meetings by observers from their respective countries. Accordingly, the Commission welcomed Mr. Francisco Linares Aranda as the observer appointed by the Government of Guatemala. At its second meeting, the Commission also agreed to authorize its officers to admit observers from any State Member of the United Nations which notified the General Secretary of its desire to send observers. From the 3rd meeting on 17 March 1965 onwards Mr. L.A.M. Lichtveld, with the consent of the officers of the Commission, attended the meeting, as observer for the Government of the Netherlands, and from the 7th meeting onward Mr. Dalibor Soldatić, Ambassador of Yugoslavia to Mexico, who was appointed as observer by his Government, was also present.

At its 2nd meeting, on 16 March 1965, the Preparatory Commission adopted its rules of procedure. The text of the rules of procedure is set out in document COPREDAL/3, dated 17 March 1965.

As a result of its discussions, the Preparatory Commission unanimously adopted the following resolutions:

RESOLUTION 1

Organization of the work of the Preparatory Commission for the Denuclearization of Latin America

The Preparatory Commission for the Denuclearization of Latin America,

Bearing in mind the provisions of resolutions I and II adopted by the Preliminary Meeting on the Denuclearization of Latin America, and in particular the task entrusted to the Commission in paragraph 2 of resolution II, namely, "to prepare a preliminary draft of a multi-lateral treaty for the denuclearization of Latin America and, to this end, to undertake the preparatory studies and measures which it considers appropriate",

Recalling that the Preliminary Meeting decided, in the same paragraph, that the Preparatory Commission for the Denuclearization of Latin America "shall constitute from its membership the working groups which it deems necessary and which shall perform their functions either at the headquarters of the Commission or elsewhere, as appropriate, and a committee to co-ordinate their work, to be called the 'Co-ordinating Committee' ",

Recalling further that the Preliminary Meeting, in paragraph 3 of the above-mentioned resolution, recommended that the Commission should give priority in its work to the matters specified in that paragraph,

Noting that, under rule 14 of its rules of procedure, the Commission agreed that "the Co-ordinating Committee shall be composed of the Chairman of the Commission, who shall preside, the two Vice-Chairmen or their representatives, and the Chairmen of the working groups or their representatives. The Commission shall delegate to the Committee such functions as it may deem appropriate",

Considering that the General Assembly of the United Nations, in its resolution 1911 (XVIII) entitled "Denuclearization of Latin America", requested the Secretary-General of the United Nations "to extend to the States of Latin America, at their request, such technical facilities as they may require in order to achieve the aims set forth in the present resolution",

Decides

I. That the Co-ordinating Committee, constituted in accordance with the provisions of rule 14 of the rules of procedure of the Preparatory Commission for the Denuclearization of Latin America, shall have its headquarters at Mexico City, and shall be responsible for the performance of the following functions and of such other functions as may hereafter be delegated to it by the Commission:

(a) Co-ordination of the work of the working groups of the Commission, and

(b) Consideration of material received from the working groups or prepared or compiled by the Committee itself, as it deems appropriate, for subsequent use in the formulation of the preliminary draft of a multilateral treaty for the denuclearization of Latin America which the Commission is instructed to prepare.

II. To establish three working groups having headquarters, membership and functions specified below:

Working Group A

Working Group A shall have its headquarters at United Nations Headquarters in New York City, shall be composed of the representatives of Argentina, Chile, Costa Rica, Ecuador, Panama and Uruguay, and shall be responsible for the performance of the following functions:

1. Definition of the geographical boundaries of the area to which the multilateral treaty to be concluded for the denuclearization of Latin America shall apply,
2. Action designed to secure the collaboration in the Commission's work of any Latin American Republic which is not yet a member of the Commission and of all other sovereign States, present or future, situated within the prospective boundaries of the area, and
3. Action designed to ensure that the extra-continental or continental States which, in addition to the Latin American Republics and the sovereign States referred to above, exercise *de jure* or *de facto* international responsibility for territories situated within the boundaries of the geographical area in question, agree to contract the same obligations with regard to those territories as the above-mentioned Republics and States contract with regard to their own, it being understood that the act of treating with the Power which at present exercises control over a given territory claimed by one of the Latin American Republics in no way prejudges the political status of that territory and cannot be interpreted in a manner prejudicial to the interests of that Republic.

Working Group B

Working Group B shall have its headquarters at Mexico City, shall be composed of the representatives of El Salvador, Haiti, Honduras, Mexico, Paraguay and Peru, and shall be responsible for effecting a study on the methods of verification, inspection and control which should be adopted to ensure the faithful fulfilment of the obligations contracted under the treaty.

Working Group C

Working Group C shall have its headquarters at United Nations Headquarters in New York City, shall be composed of the representatives of Bolivia, Brazil, Colombia, the Dominican Republic, Nicaragua and Venezuela, and shall be responsible for action designed to obtain from the nuclear Powers a commitment to the effect that they will strictly respect the legal instrument on the denuclearization of Latin America as regards all its aspects and consequences. The Latin American representatives in the Eighteen-Nation Committee on Disarmament, which meets at Geneva, shall effect liaison between the Working Group and the Committee in respect of those aspects of the Working Group's work for which such liaison may be desirable.

III. In accordance with the provisions of rules 16 and 17 of the rules of procedure of the Preparatory Commission, a majority of the members of the Co-ordinating Committee or of the Working Groups shall constitute a quorum, and shall in either case be governed by the terms of those rules of procedure.

IV. The Co-ordinating Committee may request of the Secretary-General of the United Nations such technical facilities as it may deem necessary for the better performance of its functions. The Working Groups may do likewise, through the Co-ordinating Committee, as regards their respective functions.

V. The Working Groups shall transmit to the Co-ordinating Committee on 1 July 1965 interim reports on their work, and on 1 August 1965 the reports which they are required to submit, through the Committee, to the Preparatory Commission for consideration at its second session.

VI. The Preparatory Commission shall hold its second session at Mexico City from Monday, 23 August 1965, onwards.

(Adopted at the 6th meeting, on 19 March 1965)

RESOLUTION 2

Draft resolution submitted by the Argentine Republic on the establishment of a Latin American Standing Committee on Denuclearization

The Preparatory Commission for the Denuclearization of Latin America,

Having taken cognizance, with the greatest interest, of the draft resolution submitted by the delegation of the Argentine Republic and reproduced in document COPREDAL/L/1 of 15 March 1965,

Expressing its gratitude to the delegation of the Argentine Republic for the valuable contribution which the draft resolution represents for the future progress of its work,

Considering, however, that the said draft resolution contains provisions of an executive character, since the proposed Latin American Standing Committee on Denuclearization would be responsible for "the organization, regulation, control, execution and supervision of the verification and implementation of the decisions taken by the Preparatory Commission for the Denuclearization of Latin America",

Decides

That the Argentine draft resolution shall be referred to the Co-ordinating Committee, which shall give it due consideration and shall, at such time as it deems appropriate in the light of the course of the work of the Preparatory Commission, propose its inclusion in the agenda of one of the forthcoming sessions of the Commission.

(Adopted at the 6th meeting, on 19 March 1965)

RESOLUTION 3

Vote of thanks

The Preparatory Commission for the Denuclearization of Latin America,

Considering

That the welcome extended to the Commission in Mexico by His Excellency Mr. Gustavo Díaz Ordaz and the Government of Mexico has contributed greatly to the achievement of its purposes,

That the contributions of the Chairman of the Commission, Ambassador Alfonso García Robles, and of the Vice-Chairmen, Ambassador José Sette Camara and Ambassador Rafael Eguizábal Tobías, have been most valuable,

That the secretariat of the Commission has performed its functions with great efficiency,

Decides

To address to His Excellency Mr. Gustavo Díaz Ordaz, President of the United Mexican States, an expression of its gratitude for the hospitality extended to the Commission and the impetus thus given to its work;

To congratulate Ambassador Alfonso García Robles on the results of the deliberations over which he presided, extending those congratulations also to Ambassador José Sette Camara and Ambassador Rafael Eguizábal Tobías;

To express its appreciation for the services of the General Secretary, Ambassador Carlos Peón del Valle, and his colleagues.

(Adopted at the 6th meeting, on 19 March 1965)

RESOLUTION 4

Transmission of the Final Act to the United Nations

The Preparatory Commission for the Denuclearization of Latin America

Decides

To ask the Chairman of the Commission to transmit to the Secretary-General of the United Nations the text of this Final Act, with the request that he should have it distributed as a General Assembly document for the information of Members of the United Nations in connexion with resolution 1911 (XVIII), paragraph 2.

(Adopted at the 6th meeting, on 19 March 1965)

This Final Act was unanimously adopted by the Preparatory Commission for the Denuclearization of Latin America at the closing meeting of its first session, on Monday, 22 March 1965.

16 Final Act of the Second Session of the Preparatory Commission for the Denuclearization of Latin America ▪ held in Mexico City ▪ from 23 August to 2 September 1965[4]

The second session of the Preparatory Commission for the Denuclearization of Latin America opened at Mexico City on 23 August 1965, in accordance with the provisions of section VI of resolution 1 adopted by the Commission during its first session on 19 March 1965, and closed on 2 September 1965.

The States members of the Preparatory Commission were represented at the second session as follows:

A R G E N T I N A : *Representative:* Ambassador Silvano Santander; *Alternate representative:* Mr. Samuel Daien

B O L I V I A : *Representative:* Mr. Juan José Loria; *Alternate representative:* Mr. Walter Arce Pacheco

B R A Z I L : *Representative:* Ambassador José Sette Camara; *Alternate representative:* Mr. Octavio Luiz de Berenguer César; *Adviser:* Mr. Marcos Castrioto de Azambuja

C H I L E : *Representative:* Ambassador Horacio Suárez Herreros; *Alternate representative:* Mr. Enrique Cobo del Campo

4 Reproduced in United Nations Doc. A/5985, 22 Sept. 1965.

COLOMBIA: *Representative:* Mr. Carlos Escallón Villa; *Alternate representative:* Mr. Jorge Quintero y Quintero

COSTA RICA: *Representative:* Ambassador Fernando Barrenechea; *Alternate representative:* Mr. Carlos A. Moreno; *Adviser:* Mr. Gilberto Saborío González

DOMINICAN REPUBLIC: [No representative listed.]

ECUADOR: *Representative:* Ambassador Leopoldo Benites Vinueza; *Alternate representative:* Ambassador Luis Agustín Mora Bowen; *Adviser:* Mr. Ernesto Valdivieso Chiriboga

EL SALVADOR: *Representative:* Ambassador Rafael Eguizábal Tobías

GUATEMALA: *Representative:* Ambassador Francisco Linares Aranda; *Adviser:* Mr. Juan Carlos Delpree Crespo

HAITI: *Representative:* Ambassador Julio Jean Pierre-Audain

HONDURAS: *Alternate representative:* Mr. Hernán López Callejas

MEXICO: *Representative:* Ambassador Alfonso García Robles; *Alternate representative:* Ambassador Jorge Castañeda; *Advisers:* Mr. Jesús Cabrera Muñoz-Ledo, Mr. Jaime Contreras Guerrero, Mr. Agustín Muñoz de Cote, Mr. Carlos Graef Fernández, Mr. Augusto Moreno y Moreno (alternate)

NICARAGUA: *Representative:* Ambassador Alejandro Argüello Montiel; *Alternate representative:* Mr. Edgar Escobar Fornos

PANAMA: *Representative:* Ambassador José B. Cárdenas; *Alternate representative:* Mr. Simón Quirós Guardia; *Adviser:* Mr. José B. Calvo

PARAGUAY: *Representative:* Ambassador J. Natalicio González

PERU: *Representative:* Ambassador Edgardo Seoane Corrales; *Alternate representative:* Mr. Antonio Belaúnde Moreyra

URUGUAY: *Representative:* Ambassador Enrique Rodríguez Fabregat; *Alternate representative:* Mr. Aníbal Abadie-Aicardi; *Adviser:* Mr. Alfredo Giró Pintos

VENEZUELA: *Representative:* Ambassador Rolando Salcedo Delima; *Adviser:* Mr. Virgilio Fernández

The countries listed below accredited observers to the second session as follows:

CANADA: Mr. Dwight Wilder Fulford

DENMARK: Mr. Erno Olsen

ITALY: Mr. Pio Pignatti Morano Di Custoza

JAPAN: Ambassador Kaoru Hayashi; *Alternate:* Mr. Tadashi Ohtaka

NETHERLANDS: Mr. L.A.M. Lichtveld

NORWAY: Ambassador Ernest Krogh-Hansen; *Alternate:* Mr. Sven Knudsen

SWEDEN: Mr. Arne Helleryd

UNITED KINGDOM OF GREAT BRITAIN AND NORTHERN IRELAND: Ambassador Sir Nicholas J. A. Cheetham, K.C.M.G.; *Alternate:* Mr. Thomas Christopher Barker

UNITED STATES OF AMERICA: Ambassador Fulton Freeman; *Alternate:* Mr. Charles Gordon Stefan

YUGOSLAVIA: Ambassador Dalibor Soldatić; *Alternate:* Mr. Ante Markotić

The main agenda items discussed by the Preparatory Commission were the following:

1. Report of the Co-ordinating Committee, including the reports of the Working Groups.
2. Preparation of the preliminary draft of a Multilateral Treaty for the Denuclearization of Latin America and, to that end, execution of the measures and studies referred to in resolution II of the Preliminary Meeting on the Denuclearization of Latin America.

In accordance with the appointments made during the first session, the officers of the Commission were the following:

Chairman: Ambassador Alfonso García Robles, Representative of Mexico

Vice-Chairman: Ambassador José Sette Camara, Representative of Brazil; Ambassador Rafael Eguizábal Tobías, Representative of El Salvador

Ambassador Carlos Peón del Valle, the General Secretary of the Preparatory Commission, was assisted during the second session by Mr. Antonio Gonzáles de León, Deputy Secretary, and by Mr. Sergio Gonzáles Gálvez, Mr. Joaquín Mercado and Mr. José Luis Vallarta, Assistant Secretaries.

At the 9th meeting, which was the 1st meeting of the second session, the Preparatory Commission welcomed the delegation of Guatemala to full membership, the Government of Guatemala having communicated its accession to resolution II of the Preliminary Meeting on the Denuclearization of Latin America.

At its 10th meeting the Commission decided to broaden the condition for membership laid down in resolution II of the Preliminary Meeting so that, for purposes of admission, Jamaica and Trinidad and Tobago would be subject to the same conditions as the Latin American Republics.

In addition, the Commission welcomed the presence of observers from Canada, Denmark, Italy, Japan, Norway, Sweden, the United Kingdom of Great Britain and Northern Ireland, and the United States of America, who joined the observers from the Netherlands and Yugoslavia accredited at the previous session.

At its 10th meeting, the Preparatory Commission also decided to place inter-governmental organizations on the same footing as States Members of the United Nations for the purpose of the admission of observers. The Commission agreed that, as a general rule, the Chair would allow the accredited representatives of non-governmental organizations officially registered with the United Nations to attend the Commission's proceedings, and that the Commission would deal individually with any similar applications made by other organizations which did not meet that requirement.

At the request of the Co-ordinating Committee, Mr. William Epstein, Chief of the Disarmament Affairs Group of the United Nations Secretariat, lent his valuable assistance as Technical Adviser during the second session.

In order to attend to the matters before it with due care and expedition, the Commission decided to set up a Sub-Commission with the following instructions: (1) To prepare, for submission by the Commission to the Governments of member States, a working paper based on (a) the "preliminary draft articles for the Treaty on the denuclearization of Latin America relating to verification, inspection and control", drawn up by Working Group B; (b) specific suggestions made during the Commission's proceedings, and (c) proposals submitted to the Sub-Commission by its members; and (2) To draw up recommendations to the Commission with respect to the relevant draft resolutions and agreements submitted by the Co-ordinating Committee. At the Sub-Commission's request, Working Group B also held a meeting at which it revised its preliminary draft articles on verification, inspection and control.

As a result of its discussions, the Preparatory Commission unanimously adopted the following resolutions:

RESOLUTION 5 (II)

Participation of Jamaica and Trinidad and Tobago in the Preparatory Commission

The Preparatory Commission for the Denuclearization of Latin America,

Considering that the Preliminary Meeting on the Denuclearization of Latin America, in its resolution II, agreed "To establish a Preparatory Commission for the Denuclearization of Latin America, which shall have its headquarters in Mexico and be composed of the seventeen Latin American Republics which have participated in the Meeting and those which subsequently accede to this resolution";

Bearing in mind that the Preparatory Commission, in its resolution 1, section II, decided to make Working Group A of the said Commission responsible for "Action designed to secure the collaboration in the Commission's work of any Latin American Republic which is not yet a member of the Commission and of all other sovereign States, present or future, situated within the boundaries of the area";

Taking into account the fact that Working Group A, in paragraph 10 of its report to the Co-ordinating Committee, stressed the importance of including Jamaica and Trinidad and Tobago as full members, in the proceedings of the Preparatory Commission, and

Noting that the Co-ordinating Committee, in its resolution 3, recommended that the Preparatory Commission should give priority to this question,

Decides

1. To increase the membership of the Preparatory Commission, as laid down in resolution II of the Preliminary Meeting on the Denuclearization of Latin America, by making Jamaica and Trinidad and Tobago subject to the same conditions as the Latin American Republics for the purposes of their admission to the said Preparatory Commission through accession to the above-mentioned resolution, and

2. To request the Chairman of the Preparatory Commission to transmit this resolution to the Governments of Jamaica and Trinidad and Tobago.

(Adopted at the 10th meeting, on 24 August 1965)

RESOLUTION 6 (II)

Distribution of Documents of the Preparatory Commission

The Preparatory Commission for the Denuclearization of Latin America,

Recalling that rule 23 of its rules of procedure provides that "the meetings of the Preparatory Commission shall be public unless, owing to exceptional circumstances, the said Commission decides to hold a closed meeting";

Recalling further that, each subsidiary organ of the Commission, in deciding upon its method of work, must abide by the Commission's rules of procedure, and

Considering that it is desirable for public opinion to be fully informed regarding the progress made in the work of the Commission and its subsidiary organs,

Decides

That the documents of the Preparatory Commission and its subsidiary organs shall continue to be placed in general distribution unless, owing to exceptional circumstances, the Commission or the competent subsidiary organ decides otherwise.

(Adopted at the 16th meeting, on 31 August 1965)

RESOLUTION 7 (II)

Establishment of a Negotiating Committee

The Preparatory Commission for the Denuclearization of Latin America,

Having examined the reports of Working Groups A and C transmitted to it by the Co-ordinating Committee;

Bearing in mind that, as emphasized in the debates of the Eighteen-Nation Disarmament Committee, the prevention of the dissemination or proliferation of nuclear weapons becomes a matter of greater urgency with every passing day;

Considering therefore that it would be highly desirable to take the opportunity afforded by the United Nations General Assembly's twentieth session for action towards the attainment of the objectives pursued by the said Working Groups, and

Noting that the work done by the two Working Groups demonstrates the close relationship in certain respects, between the questions with which they have to deal,

Decides

1. To establish a Negotiating Committee composed of the Chairman of the Preparatory Commission and the Chairmen—or, in their absence, the Vice-Chairmen—of Working Groups A and C;
2. To instruct the said Committee to endeavour while the United Nations General Assembly's twentieth session is in progress in New York City, to expedite to the utmost, through negotiations with authorized representatives of the States concerned, the fulfilment of the purposes defined in section II of resolution 1, adopted by the Preparatory Commission on 19 March 1965, and
3. To request the Negotiating Committee to consult Working Groups A and C whenever it deems this advisable, to keep them informed of the progress of its work, and to submit to the Preparatory Commission through the Co-ordinating Committee, at the appropriate time, a report on the progress and results of that work.

(Adopted at the 16th meeting, on 31 August 1965)

RESOLUTION 8 (II)

Preamble of the preliminary draft of a Multilateral Treaty for the Denuclearization of Latin America

The Preparatory Commission for the Denuclearization of Latin America,

Having considered the working paper prepared by the Secretariat pursuant to the agreement reached by the Co-ordinating Committee and submitted to the Commission in document COPREDAL/S/DT/1, and

Taking into account the proposals submitted and the views expressed in the debate on the said working paper,

Decides

To approve the following text as a declaration of the principles which shall serve as a basis for the Preamble of the preliminary draft of a Multilateral Treaty for the Denuclearization of Latin America:

In the name of their peoples and faithfully interpreting their desires and aspirations, the Governments represented at the Conference of Plenipotentiaries for the Denuclearization of Latin America,

Desiring to contribute, so far as lies in their power, towards ending the armaments race, especially in nuclear weapons, and towards strengthening a world at peace, based on the sovereign equality of States, mutual respect and good neighbourliness;

Recalling that the United Nations General Assembly, in its resolution 808 (IX), adopted unanimously as one of the three points of a co-ordinated programme of disarmament "The total prohibition of the use and manufacture of nuclear weapons and weapons of mass destruction of every type, together with the conversion of existing stocks of nuclear weapons for peaceful purposes", and

Recalling also United Nations General Assembly resolution 1911 (XVIII), which established that the measures that should be agreed upon for the denuclearization of Latin America should be taken "in the light of the principles of the Charter of the United Nations and of regional agreements";

Convinced:

That the incalculable destructive power of nuclear weapons has made it imperative that the legal prohibition of war should be strictly observed in practice if the survival of civilization and of mankind itself is to be assured;

That nuclear weapons, whose terrible effects are suffered, without distinction and without escape, by the armies and by the civilian population alike, constitute, through the persistence of the radioactivity they release, an attack on the integrity of the human species and ultimately may even render the whole Earth uninhabitable;

That general and complete disarmament under effective international control is a vital matter which all the peoples of the world equally demand;

That the proliferation of nuclear weapons, which seems inevitable unless States, in the exercise of their sovereign rights, use self-restraint in order to prevent it, would make any agreement on disarmament enormously more difficult and would increase the danger of the outbreak of a nuclear conflagration;

That the privileged situation of the States represented at the Conference, whose territories are wholly free from nuclear weapons and their launching devices, imposes upon them the inescapable duty, of preserving that situation both in their own interests and for the good of mankind;

That the existence of nuclear weapons in any country of Latin America would make it a target for possible nuclear attacks and would inevitably set off, throughout the region, a ruinous race in nuclear weapons which would involve the unjustifiable diversion, for warlike purposes, of the limited resources available for economic and social development;

That the foregoing factors, coupled with the traditional peace-loving outlook of their peoples, make it essential that nuclear energy should be used in Latin America exclusively for peaceful purposes.

That the denuclearization of vast geographical areas, adopted by the

94

sovereign decision of the States comprised therein, will exercise a beneficial influence on other regions;

Convinced, finally:

That the denuclearization of the States represented at the Conference—being understood to mean the undertaking entered into internationally in this Treaty to keep their territories free for ever, as they have been hitherto, from nuclear weapons and their launching devices—will constitute a measure of protection for their peoples against the squandering of their limited resources on nuclear armaments and against possible nuclear attacks upon their territories; a significant contribution towards preventing the proliferation of nuclear weapons; and a powerful factor for general and complete disarmament; and

That Latin America, faithful to its deep-seated tradition of universality of outlook, must endeavour not only to banish from its homelands the scourge of a nuclear war and to strive for the well-being and advancement of its peoples, but also, at the same time, to co-operate in the fulfilment of the ideals of mankind, that is to say in the consolidation of a lasting peace based on equal rights, economic fairness and social justice for all, in accordance with the principles and purposes of the Charter of the United Nations,

Have agreed as follows:

(Adopted at the 16th meeting, on 31 August 1965)

RESOLUTION 9 (II)

Preliminary draft articles on verification, inspection and control

The Preparatory Commission for the Denuclearization of Latin America,

Having considered with especial appreciation the preliminary draft articles for the Treaty on the Denuclearization of Latin America relating to verification, inspection and control, drawn up by Working Group B and submitted to the Preparatory Commission by the Co-ordinating Committee, and

Taking into account the fact that the highly technical nature of some of the provisions of the said preliminary draft makes it necessary for them to be studied by the member States,

Decides:

1. To transmit to the Governments of the member States, for study, the preliminary draft articles for the Treaty on the Denuclearization of Latin America which appear as an annex to this resolution;
2. To recommend that the Governments shall transmit their observa-

tions on the said preliminary draft to the General Secretary as soon as possible and in any case no later than 15 January 1966; requesting them to arrange, so far as possible, for the said observations to be presented in a suitable form for direct use in the preparation of the articles of the Treaty;

3. To request the Co-ordinating Committee to prepare, on the basis of the preliminary draft articles annexed to this resolution and of such observations as the Governments may make, a working paper for use in drafting a new version of the preliminary draft;

4. To request the Co-ordinating Committee to transmit to the Governments, by 28 February 1966 at the latest, the working paper referred to in paragraph 3 of this resolution, and

5. To express its gratitude to the General Secretary and to the United Nations Technical Adviser for their contribution to the Commission's work.

COPREDAL/19

ANNEX

TREATY FOR THE DENUCLEARIZATION OF LATIN AMERICA: PRELIMINARY
DRAFT ARTICLES RELATING TO VERIFICATION, INSPECTION AND CONTROL*

Introduction

The articles relating to verification, inspection and control prepared by Working Group B were drafted not with the aim of securing the Preparatory Commission's immediate approval but as a working document and starting-point for the study of this matter.

The objectives of the proposed system are as follows:

(a) to prohibit the manufacture and acquisition of nuclear weapons by any country of Latin America;

(b) to prevent the introduction or deployment of nuclear weapons in any country of Latin America by any nuclear Power; and

(c) to ensure that the aforesaid prohibitions do not in any way impede the use of nuclear energy for peaceful purposes.

The system of verification, inspection and control outlined in the preliminary draft articles for the Treaty is designed to be:

(a) as simple as possible to install and operate;

(b) as inexpensive as possible; and

* This document concentrates exclusively on the aspects of the Treaty which are clearly related to the matters assigned to Working Group B.

(c) as effective as possible in preventing any violation or evasion of the obligations of the Treaty. For this purpose, the proposed system is based mainly on the Revised Safeguards System of the International Atomic Energy Agency.

The aim of the preliminary draft articles is not to present the entire outline of the treaty but simply to set forth the minimum provisions for determining the nature of the control organization to be set up; consequently, other provisions will naturally have to be added in order to produce a treaty in its final form.

Preamble

. . . . .

A r t i c l e A

Obligations

(1) The Contracting Parties hereby undertake, in regard to their respective territories, to prohibit and prevent:

(a) the testing, use, manufacture, production or acquisition by any means whatsoever of any nuclear weapon, by the Parties themselves or by anyone on their behalf; and

(b) the receipt, storage, installation, deployment, and any form of possession of any nuclear weapon, by the Parties themselves or by anyone on their behalf.

(2) The Parties also undertake to refrain from engaging in, promoting, encouraging, directly or indirectly, or in any way participating in the testing, use, manufacture, production, possession or control of any nuclear weapon inside or outside their territory.

Commentary:

The main purpose of the obligations which the member States would assume, on the basis of this article, is to prevent the proliferation of nuclear weapons by banning them from the countries of Latin America. This same article establishes the prohibitions and limitations required to keep Latin America denuclearized.

Although the substance of the article is not directly concerned with the system of verification, inspection and control, its inclusion was considered necessary in order to clarify the obligations whose fulfilment would be verified.

It was considered that the obligations which the Parties would assume under this article would not affect or conflict with any obligations assumed by member States under the Charter of the United Nations or under regional agreements.

97

Article B

Definition of "territory"

For the purposes of this Treaty, the term "territory" shall be understood to include the territorial sea and air space.

Commentary:

It was considered necessary to include this article in order to specify that the term "territory" includes the territorial sea and air space of each country, although no attempt has been made to define the scope of the term "territorial sea" because of the different positions of member States in this matter. This question could be left to the interpretation of each member State or some definition could be agreed on, for the purposes of the Treaty, by the Contracting Parties.

Article C

Definition of "nuclear weapons"

(1) For the purposes of this Treaty, a nuclear weapon is defined as any weapon which contains, or is designed to utilize, nuclear fuel or radioactive isotopes and which, by explosion or other uncontrolled transformation of the nuclear fuel or radioactive isotopes, is capable of mass destruction, mass injury or mass poisoning;

(2) Furthermore, any part, device, assembly or material especially designed for, or primarily useful in, any weapon as set forth under paragraph (1) of this article or in any vehicle or system especially designed for the launching of such weapons shall be deemed to be a nuclear weapon;

(3) Nuclear fuel as used in the preceding definition includes plutonium, Uranium 233, Uranium 235 (including Uranium contained in Uranium enriched to over 2.1 per cent by weight of Uranium 235) and any other material capable of releasing substantial quantities of nuclear energy through fission, fusion or other nuclear reaction of the material. The foregoing materials shall be considered to be nuclear fuel regardless of the physical or chemical form in which they exist. Material which exceeds the limits set in article 24 of the Revised Safeguards System of the International Atomic Energy Agency shall be considered to be material capable of releasing substantial quantities of nuclear energy.

Commentary:

The definition of a "nuclear weapon" includes both the nuclear explosive and the launching device. This definition was taken from the Protocol on the Control of Armaments of the Treaty of the Western European Union, signed in Paris on 23 October 1954, whereby the Federal Republic of Germany undertook not to manufacture in its territory any atomic weapons, chemical weapons or biological weapons.

A r t i c l e   D

Organization of control

(1) In order to ensure fulfilment of the obligations assumed under this Treaty, there is hereby established a Centre* (hereinafter referred to as "the Centre"), which shall operate in accordance with the provisions of this Treaty and the annexes thereto.

(2) The Parties agree to extend to the Centre full and prompt co-operation in accordance with the provisions of this Treaty, of any agreements they may conclude with the Centre, and of any agreements the Centre may conclude with the International Atomic Energy Agency or with any other international organization.

A r t i c l e   E

Organs of control

The organs of the Centre shall be a Conference of the Parties (hereinafter referred to as "the Conference") and an administrative official (hereinafter referred to as "the Director"), assisted by the necessary technical and administrative staff.

Commentary:

The intention of these articles is to establish an agency which will be small in size and easy to operate and whose principal functions will include supervision of the application of the system of verification, inspection and control.

A r t i c l e   F

The Conference

The Conference shall establish the procedures of the control system for the observance of this Treaty, in accordance with the provisions of the Treaty and of the annexes thereto.

* Term used without prejudice to the definitive term to be adopted.

Commentary:

The "Conference" of the member States, which would probably meet once a year, would be the principal body responsible for the functioning of the system as a whole. This article only mentions the Conference's duties with respect to the control system and does so in very general terms. The Treaty should, of course, include a series of constitutional and procedural provisions that would supplement the provisions in this article.

A r t i c l e   G

The Director

(1) The Director shall be the chief administrative official of the Centre and head of the staff. He shall be responsible to the Conference and, under its supervision, shall execute its policy directives. He shall be responsible for the operation of the control system in accordance with the provisions of this Treaty and with the procedures established by the Conference. He shall provide the Conference with whatever advice, reports and assistance it may require for the performance of its functions. He shall, if the Conference so requests, recommend rules for the approval of the Conference regarding the appointment, organization and operation of the staff of the Centre.

(2) The Director shall establish the procedures for distributing, to all Parties, all information materials the Centre may receive from governmental or non-governmental sources.

(3) The Director shall submit to the Conference an annual report and such special reports as he may deem appropriate. From time to time, he shall submit to the Conference recommendations concerning the adoption of measures for improving the control system.

Commentary:

This article seems to be self-explanatory as regards the Director's relationship with the Conference and the powers that would enable the Director to discharge his duties as effectively as possible. In addition, it would make it possible to organize a relatively small staff, in the light of the nature of nuclear development in Latin America. It is understood that an Assistant Director would be appointed to assume the duties of the Director during his absence, and that the staff would have the status of international civil servants.

Article H

The IAEA Safeguards System

(1) The Parties shall assume all the obligations and adopt all the procedures of the International Atomic Energy Agency's Safeguards System, as revised on 25 February 1965, with regard to any nuclear facilities and activities in their respective territories, including any gaseous diffusion plant, centrifuge plant, chemical separation or reprocessing plant and any other plant for the production, refining or utilization of fissionable material. The said Safeguards System is annexed to this Treaty as annex . . . . .

(2) Any revision or subsequent amendment of the IAEA Safeguards System shall be equally binding upon and applicable to the Parties as if it were incorporated in the present text, when approved by the Conference.

Commentary:

This article establishes the fundamental system on which the method of verification, inspection and control in question is based. The IAEA's Revised Safeguards System, which was unanimously approved by that body's Board of Governors on 25 February 1965 and the text of which is annexed hereto, provides for a comprehensive reporting and inspection machinery, not only with regard to power and research reactors but also with regard to all the facilities for preparing or processing nuclear materials. Moreover, the possibility has been borne in mind that IAEA might share responsibility for the implementation and cost of this system.

Article I

Reports of the Parties

(1) The Parties shall simultaneously transmit to the Centre a copy of any report which they may submit to IAEA.

(2) The Parties shall submit to the Centre semi-annual reports stating that no activity prohibited under this Treaty has occurred in their respective territories or on their behalf in any other place.

Commentary:

This article would guarantee that the official information received, on a world-wide basis, by the IAEA from all signatory States is made available to the Contracting States.

A r t i c l e J
Special reports requested by the Director

(1) Whenever he deems this desirable, the Director may request any of the Parties to provide the Centre with complementary or supplementary information, data or clarifications regarding any suspicious event or circumstance, and the Parties undertake to co-operate with him promptly and fully in complying with such requests.

(2) The Director shall inform all Parties forthwith of such requests and of the respective replies.

Commentary:

This article supplements the information procedures which IAEA has found necessary in order to ensure the effectiveness of the system.

A r t i c l e K
Special inspections

(1) Special inspections may be carried out in the following circumstances:

(a) By the IAEA in accordance with the provisions of its Safeguards System;

(b) If so requested by any Party that suspects that some prohibited activity has taken place, is taking place or is about to take place, in the territory of any other Party or anywhere on such latter Party's behalf. The Director shall take immediate steps to arrange for the carrying out of such inspection;

(c) If so requested by any Party who is suspected or accused of having violated the Treaty. The Director shall take immediate steps to arrange for the carrying out of such inspection.

(2) The costs and expenses of any special inspection carried out under paragraph 1, sub-paragraph (b) or (c), of this article shall be borne by the requesting Party or Parties, except where the report on the special inspection concludes that, in view of the relevant circumstances, such costs and expenses should not be borne by the requesting Party or Parties.

(3) The Conference shall formulate the procedures for the organization and execution of any special inspections that may be carried out in accordance with paragraph 1, sub-paragraphs (b) and (c) of this article.

(4) The Parties shall undertake to grant the inspectors carrying out such special inspections full and free access to whatever places and information they may require for the performance of their duties. If so requested by the authorities of the Party in whose territory the inspection is carried out, the inspectors appointed by the Conference shall be accompanied by representatives of the said authorities, provided that this does not in any way delay or hinder the inspectors in the performance of their duties.

(5) The Director shall immediately transmit to all the Parties a copy of any report pursuant to any special inspection.

(6) Similarly, the Director shall immediately send to the Secretary-General of the United Nations, for the information of the Security Council and the General Assembly, a copy of any report pursuant to any special inspection.

(7) The Director, or any of the Parties, may request a special session of the Conference for the purpose of considering the report pursuant to any special inspection. The Director shall convene a special session of the Conference when so requested by any Party to this Treaty.

(8) The Conference, convened in special session under this article, may make recommendations to the Parties and also submit reports to the Secretary-General of the United Nations for the information of the Security Council and the General Assembly.

Commentary:

An attempt has been made in this article to supplement the IAEA Safeguards System by providing for procedures deemed appropriate when the objective sought is not limited to preventing the diversion of nuclear materials to military use but covers the prohibition of nuclear weapons in those territories covered by the Safeguards System.

To that end, the article includes elements designed to deter possible violation by providing for the possibility of carrying out special inspections and, moreover, by helping to ensure a full and timely clarification of the facts whenever deliberate or involuntary violations are suspected. Lastly, it should be stressed that there is ample reason to believe that the measures provided for under this article will need to be used only very rarely, in view of the special characteristics of Latin America.

A r t i c l e   L

Explosions for peaceful purposes

(1) The Parties agree not to explode nuclear devices for peaceful purposes or to give assistance to third parties to that end, except in

accordance with the present article and the Treaty banning nuclear weapon tests in the atmosphere, in outer space and under water, signed in Moscow on 5 August 1963 and any amendments thereto. Explosions which are carried out in compliance with the present article shall not be deemed to constitute violations of article A of this Treaty.

(2) Parties intending to carry out or co-operate in the carrying out of such an explosion, shall first apply for and obtain authorization from the Centre. In its application such Party shall submit to the Centre, four months prior to the date of the proposed explosion, a plan containing the following information:

    (a) the nature of the nuclear device and the source from which it was obtained;

    (b) the date, place and purpose of the proposed explosion;

    (c) the procedures which will be followed in order to comply with paragraph 4 of this article;

    (d) the anticipated yield of the device; and

    (e) the measures which will be taken to ensure that there will be no substantial radioactive fall-out outside the immediate vicinity.

(3) The Conference may authorize, at either a regular or a special session, explosions proposed in accordance with the present article,

(4) Members of the staff of the Centre and of IAEA shall be empowered to observe all the preparations for and the explosion of the device and shall have unrestricted access at all times to the vicinity of the explosion, in order to ascertain whether the device and procedures followed during the explosion are in conformity with the information submitted in accordance with paragraph 2 of the present article.

Commentary:

The purposes of this article are to ensure: (a) that this Treaty in no way impedes operations for the peaceful use of nuclear energy; and (b) that no explosion for peaceful purposes is used to secure military advantages.

The use of nuclear energy for peaceful purposes would therefore not be affected by the prohibitions of the Treaty. This article refers only to nuclear explosions involving the use of devices similar to those used in nuclear weapons. By way of precedent, it should be pointed out that, at the Conference on the Discontinuance of Nuclear Weapons Tests, held in 1960, it was considered necessary to include such an article, because, if it were omitted, all nuclear explosions would be prohibited.

Article M

Relations with other organizations

The Conference, in addition to its power to approve any agreements that may be concluded between the Centre and the International Atomic Energy Agency, shall take whatever steps are necessary for the Centre to enter into an appropriate relationship with any international organization which may be established in the future to supervise disarmament or measures for the control of armaments in any part of the world.

Commentary:

This article empowers the Conference to approve any agreement of association that may be concluded between the Centre and IAEA and to lay down guidelines with regard to the relations between the former and other organizations with similar aims, since the Conference is considered to be the most representative organ of the Centre.

Article N

Measures in the event of violation of the Treaty

Should the Conference determine that any Party is not complying fully with its obligations under this Treaty, the Conference shall report thereon to the Security Council and to the General Assembly through the Secretary-General of the United Nations, and may consider the question of relieving any other Party or Parties of their obligations under this Treaty, on such conditions and for such period as the Conference may determine.

Commentary:

If, in the opinion of the Conference, there is a violation of the Treaty, there will, in fact, be no economic or military sanctions which the Centre itself could impose. This article accordingly prescribes two measures likely to have a decisive effect on the prevention of violations: firstly, it provides that the question is to be reported to the Security Council and to the General Assembly of the United Nations as a matter which may endanger international peace and security; and, secondly, it provides that the Conference may consider the question of relieving of its or their obligations, on such conditions and for such period as the Conference itself may determine, and the member State or States which feel themselves threatened. It is to be hoped that this article would be applied only on rare occasions and it has been included merely as a precaution.

(Approved at the 17th meeting, held on 31 August 1965)

RESOLUTION 10 (II)
THIRD SESSION OF THE PREPARATORY COMMISSION

The Preparatory Commission for the Denuclearization of Latin America,

Recalling that the General Assembly of the United Nations, in resolution 1911 (XVIII) of 27 November 1963, recognized "the need to preserve, in Latin America, conditions which will prevent the countries of the region from becoming involved in a dangerous and ruinous nuclear arms race",

Noting that, as the deliberations of the United Nations Disarmament Commission and of the Eighteen-Nation Disarmament Committee show, the need to prevent the proliferation of nuclear weapons is daily becoming more urgent,

Reaffirming the recommendations made to the Preparatory Commission by the Preliminary Meeting on the Denuclearization of Latin America in paragraph 3 of its resolution II, which was adopted on 27 November 1964,

Considering that the Preparatory Commission, directly and through its subsidiary organs, has already made substantial progress towards completing the work assigned to it in the above-mentioned resolution II,

Bearing in mind that the principal nuclear Powers have publicly and repeatedly declared themselves in favour of regional denuclearization, as a means of facilitating universal denuclearization under a programme of general and complete disarmament under effective international control,

Mindful that the people of Latin America desire the speedy and complete success of the work of the Preparatory Commission,

Decides

1. To set Tuesday, 19 April 1966, as the date of the first meeting of the Third Session of the Preparatory Commission for the Denuclearization of Latin America;
2. To call upon the Governments of member States to redouble their efforts to enable the Preparatory Commission to draw up, during its Third Session, the preliminary draft of a treaty for the denuclearization of Latin America, in accordance with the instructions given

106

to it by the Preliminary Meeting on the Denuclearization of Latin America in 1964;

3. To call upon those Governments to take such measures as they deem appropriate to achieve the purpose described in the preceding paragraph.

(Approved at the 17th meeting, held on 31 August 1965)

RESOLUTION 11 (II)

VOTE OF THANKS

The Preparatory Commission for the Denuclearization of Latin America,

Considering

That the Government of the United Mexican States, under the Presidency of His Excellency Mr. Gustavo Díaz Ordaz, enthusiastically upholds the noble ideals of peace, understanding and the defence of the peoples of Latin America against the threat of destruction or debilitation which would result from manufacturing, receiving, storing or testing nuclear weapons or nuclear launching devices;

The lucidity, efficiency and dedication with which the Chairman, Ambassador Alfonso García Robles, has brought the work of the Second Session to a successful conclusion;

The incomparable efficiency and constant zeal with which the secretariat of the Commission has performed its duties,

Decides

1. To express to His Excellency President Gustavo Díaz Ordaz and to His Excellency Mr. Antonio Carrillo Flores, Minister for Foreign Affairs, its deep gratitude for the welcome and encouragement given to the Commission;
2. To congratulate Ambassador Alfonso García Robles on the results of the deliberations over which he presided; and
3. To express to Ambassador Carlos Peón del Valle, General Secretary, and to Mr. Antonio González de León, Assistant Secretary of the Commission, and his colleagues, its gratitude for their tireless efforts, which ensured the success of its work.

(Adopted at the 18th meeting, held on 2 September 1965)

This Final Act was unanimously adopted by the Preparatory Commission for the Denuclearization of Latin America at the closing meeting of its second session, held on Wednesday, 2 September 1965.

17 Final Act of the Third Session of the Preparatory Commission for the Denuclearization of Latin America ▪ held in Mexico City ▪ from 19 April to 4 May 1966[5]

In accordance with resolution 10 (II), adopted on 31 August 1965, the Preparatory Commission for the Denuclearization of Latin America held its third session from 19 April to 4 May 1966.

The States members of the Preparatory Commission were represented at this session as follows:

ARGENTINA: *Representative:* Mr. Luis Santiago Sanz, Ambassador; *Alternate representatives:* Mr. Julio César Carasales, Mr. Vicente Ernesto Berasategui; *Advisers:* Mr. Mario Eduardo Báncora, Mr. Alberto Santiago Insúa, Mr. Rómulo Victor Trombetta

BOLIVIA: *Representative:* Mr. Mario Ovando Ovando; *Alternate representative:* Mr. Francisco J. Santiago

BRAZIL: *Representative:* Mr. José Sette Camara, Ambassador; *Alternate representatives:* Mr. Paulo Ribeiro Arruda, Mr. Fernando Guimarães de Cerqueira Lima; *Advisers:* Mr. Carlos Antonio B. Bueno, Mr. Marcos C. de Azambuja

CHILE: *Representative:* Mr. Gonzalo Latorre Salamanca, Ambassador; *Alternate representatives:* Mr. Mario Rodríguez Altamirano,

[5] Reproduced in United Nations Doc. A/6328, 12 May 1966. Above text corrected by author.

Ambassador, Mr. Armando Uribe Arce; *Adviser:* Mr. Enrique Cobo del Campo

C O L O M B I A : *Representative:* Mr. César Augusto Pantoja, Ambassador; *Alternate representatives:* Mr. Tulio A. Marulanda, Mr. Jorge Cervantes Pinzón

C O S T A R I C A : *Representative:* Mr. Francisco Alvarez Monge; *Alternate representatives:* Mr. Gilberto Saborío González, Mrs. Carmen Herdocia de Hernández

D O M I N I C A N R E P U B L I C : *Representative:* Mr. René Fiallo; *Alternate representative:* Mr. Leonte Guzmán Vidal

E C U A D O R : *Representative:* Mr. Leopoldo Benites Vinueza, Ambassador; *Alternate representative:* Mr. Ernesto Valdivieso Chiriboga

E L S A L V A D O R : *Representative:* Mr. Rafael Eguizábal Tobías, Ambassador; *Alternate representative:* Mr. Guillermo Rubio Melhado

G U A T E M A L A : *Representative:* Mr. Carlos García Bauer, Ambassador; *Alternate representatives:* Mr. Francisco Linares Aranda, Ambassador, Mr. Rolando Ureta Laparra

H A I T I : *Representative*: Mr. Julio Jean Pierre-Audain, Ambassador

H O N D U R A S : *Representative:* Mr. Armando Veláquez Cerrato, Ambassador; *Alternate representative:* Mr. Hernán López Callejas; *Adviser:* Mr. Roberto Alonzo Cleaves

J A M A I C A : *Representative:* Mr. Frederick E. Degazon, O.B.E.; *Alternate representative:* Mr. Lloyd M. H. Barnett

M E X I C O : *Representative:* Mr. Alfonso García Robles, Ambassador; *Alternate representative:* Mr. Jorge Castañeda, Ambassador; *Advisers:* Mr. Jesús Cabrera Muñoz-Ledo, Mr. Roberto de Rosenzweig-Díaz A., Mr. Joaquín Mercado, Mr. Jaime Contreras Guerrero, Mr. Agustín Muñoz de Cote, Mr. Carlos Graef Fernández, Mr. Roberto Treviño

N I C A R A G U A : *Representative:* Mr. Alejandro Argüello Montiel, Ambassador; *Alternate representatives:* Mr. Edgar Escobar Fornos, Mr. Gilberto Pérez Alonso

P A N A M A : *Representative:* Mr. José B. Cárdenas, Ambassador; *Alternate representatives:* Mr. Simón Quirós Guardia, Mr. José B. Calvo

P A R A G U A Y : *Representative:* Mr. Bacon Duarte Prado, Ambassador

P E R U : *Representative:* Mr. Edgardo Seoane Corrales, Ambassador; *Alternate representatives:* Mr. Felipe Portocarrero Olave, Ambassador; Mr. Carlos Silva Morón

TRINIDAD AND TOBAGO: *Representative:* Sir Ellis Clarke, Ambassador

URUGUAY: *Representative:* Mrs. María E. Rocha de Barthaburu; *Alternate representatives:* Mr. Aníbal Abadie-Aicardi, Mr. Alfredo Giró Pintos

VENEZUELA: *Representative:* Mr. Rolando Salcedo Delima, Ambassador; *Alternate representatives:* Mr. Augusto Brito Ascanio, Mr. José Alberto Velandia; *Advisers:* Mr. Virgilio Fernández, Mrs. María Cristina Gómez de Sucre

The Preparatory Commission was assisted at this session by Mr. William Epstein, Chief of the Disarmament Affairs Division of the United Nations Secretariat, who acted as Technical Adviser.

The following observers attended this session of the Preparatory Commission:

AUSTRIA: Mr. Hans Thalberg, Ambassador; *Alternate:* Mr. Herbert Grubmayr

CANADA: Mr. Dwight Wilder Fulford

DENMARK: Mr. Erno M. Olsen

FEDERAL REPUBLIC OF GERMANY: Mr. Swidbert Schnippenkötter, Ambassador; *Alternate:* Mr. Jürgen Diesel

FRANCE: Mr. Jacques Vimont, Ambassador; *Alternate:* Mr. Henri de Coignac

INDIA: Mr. Naranjan Singh Gill, Ambassador; *Alternate:* Mr. C. Dasgupta

ITALY: Mr. Enrico Guastone Belcredi, Ambassador; *Alternate:* Mr. Pio Pignatti Morano di Custoza

JAPAN: Mr. Shiro Ishiguro, Ambassador; *Alternate:* Mr. Yoji Sugiyama

NETHERLANDS: Mr. L.A.M. Lichtveld, Ambassador

NORWAY: Mr. Nils Oskar Dietz

POLAND: Mr. Jerzy Grudzinski, Ambassador

SWEDEN: Mr. Arne Helleryd

UNITED ARAB REPUBLIC: Mr. Hassan Salah El Din Gohar, Ambassador; *Alternate:* Mr. Abdel Rahman Hassan

UNITED KINGDOM OF GREAT BRITAIN AND NORTHERN IRELAND: Sir Nicholas J.A. Cheetham, Ambassador; *Alternate:* Mr. Thomas C. Barker

UNITED STATES OF AMERICA: Mr. Fulton Freeman, Ambassador; *Alternate:* Mr. Charles Gordon Stefan

YUGOSLAVIA: Mr. Dalibor Soldatić, Ambassador; *Alternate:* Mr. Ante Markotić

INTER-AMERICAN NUCLEAR ENERGY COMMISSION: Mr. Enrique Ferrer Vieyra

INTERNATIONAL ATOMIC ENERGY AGENCY: Mr. Reinhard Rainer

At the session, the Preparatory Commission had the following item on its agenda:

Preparation of the preliminary draft of a Multilateral Treaty for the Denuclearization of Latin America.

The Commission's debates and activities were based on the following documents: the working paper which the Co-ordinating Committee submitted to the Preparatory Commission for drawing up the preliminary draft of a Treaty on the Denuclearization of Latin America (COPREDAL/CC/DT/1 and Corr.); the report of the Negotiating Committee (COPREDAL/CN/1); the report of the Co-ordinating Committee, dated 14 March 1966 (COPREDAL/CC/20 and annexes); the draft Treaty on the Denuclearization of Latin America, submitted by the delegations of Brazil and Colombia (COPREDAL/L/13); and the proposals submitted by delegations (COPREDAL/S/20/Rev. 2 and Add.1).

As at the previous sessions, the Officers of the Commission were the following:

Chairman: Mr. Alfonso García Robles, Ambassador, Representative of Mexico

Vice-Chairmen: Mr. José Sette Camara, Ambassador, Representative of Brazil, Mr. Rafael Eguizábal Tobías, Ambassador, Representative of El Salvador

Mr. Carlos Péon del Valle, Ambassador, acted as General Secretary of the Preparatory Commission. He was assisted by Mr. Antonio González de Léon, Deputy Secretary; Mr. Manuel Tello Macías, Mr. Sergio González Gálvez, and Mr. José Luis Vallarta, Assistant Secretaries; and Mr. José Pontones Tovar, who acted as Co-ordinator.

Just before the third session began, the Governments of Trinidad and Tobago and Jamaica informed the Chairman of the Preparatory Commission of their accession to resolution II of the Preliminary Meeting on the Denuclearization of Latin America. The Commission accordingly welcomed the representatives of those countries at its 20th and 21st meetings respectively. As a result, the Preparatory Commission decided unanimously, on the proposal of its Secretariat, to revise rule 20 of its rules of procedure (COPREDAL/3) so as to make English an official language.

The Preparatory Commission also welcomed the observers for Austria, the Federal Republic of Germany, France, India, Poland and the United Arab Republic, who joined the observers already accredited at previous sessions. The session was also attended by observers for the International Atomic Energy Agency and the Inter-American Nuclear Energy Commission.

Apart from the resolutions adopted at this session, which are reproduced below, the Preparatory Commission agreed on 3 May 1966, at its 33rd meeting, on the following:

(a) To recommend that the Governments of member States, in the light of the statements made at the 32nd meeting, should study the question of transit raised by the delegation of Nicaragua, so that efforts may be made to reach a conclusion on the subject at the next session;

(b) To recognize the importance of the proposal made by the delegation of Uruguay that the Governments of member States should make all the necessary efforts "to arrive at an accurate geographical demarcation of the area which is to have denuclearized status, with the necessary assistance of specialized technical personnel" and to recommend that Governments themselves should study this recommendation carefully;

(c) To postpone consideration of the annexes to the report of the Coordinating Committee until the fourth session, not having had an opportunity to consider them at the third.

The delegations of Argentina, Bolivia, Brazil, Colombia, the Dominican Republic, Panama, Peru and Venezuela stated that they reserved the right to seek, at such time as they saw fit, the views of the competent organs of the Inter-American System on the establishment of a denuclearized zone in Latin America, in the light of the regional agreements in force and the documents prepared by the Preparatory Commission.

At its 34th meeting, the Commission passed a vote of thanks to the Secretary-General of the United Nations for the encouraging message (COPREDAL/S/INf.33) which he sent to the Commission on 19 April, on the occasion of the opening of the third session, and for the valuable services of Mr. William Epstein, United Nations Technical Adviser.

In order to facilitate and expedite the work of the session, the Preparatory Commission established, to start with, two working groups: Group I on the technical problems involved in the proposed Treaty; and Group II on the problems of continental security it raises. The Chairman of Group I was Mr. Armando Uribe Arce (Chile) and the Rapporteur was Mr. José Alberto Velandía (Venezuela). The Chairman of Group II was Mr. Felipe Portocarrero (Peru), and the Rapporteur was Mr. Vicente Ernesto Berasategui (Argentina). Later, it was found necessary to set up an *Ad Hoc* Group and a new Technical Group, which considered various items on which the Commission had not yet reached agreement. The Chairman of the *Ad Hoc* Group was Mr. José Sette Câmara (Brazil) and the Chairman of the Technical Group was Mr. Armando Uribe Arce.

As a result of the work of these groups and of its discussions in plenary session, the Preparatory Commission reached unanimity on the following resolutions:

RESOLUTION 12 (III)

REPORT OF THE NEGOTIATING COMMITTEE

The Preparatory Commission for the Denuclearization of Latin America,

Having examined the report of the Negotiating Committee (CO-PREDAL/CN/1), which was of practical use in connexion with the relevant aspects of the Commission's work,

Noting that the Negotiating Committee was unable to make contact at United Nations Headquarters, New York, with representatives of the Government of the People's Republic of China,

Decides

1. *To express* its gratitude to the members of the Negotiating Committee for the excellent work they accomplished during the twentieth session of the United Nations General Assembly in carrying out the work assigned to them by the Preparatory Commission;

2. *To request* the Negotiating Committee to make informal inquiries, in the manner and by the means it deems fit, to ascertain whether the Government of the People's Republic of China would be prepared to undertake to respect the legal instrument on the denuclearization of Latin America;

3. *To request* the Negotiating Committee, also, to transmit to the Governments of member States a report on the results of its efforts before the opening of the Commission's fourth session.

(Adopted at the 33rd meeting, on 3 May 1966)

RESOLUTION 13 (III)

REPORT OF THE CO-ORDINATING COMMITTEE

The Preparatory Commission for the Denuclearization of Latin America,

Having considered the report of the Co-ordinating Committee (CO-PREDAL/CC/20) and the documents annexed thereto, particularly the working paper (COPREDAL/CC/DT/1) dated 14 March 1966, which the Committee transmitted to the Governments of member States and submitted to the Commission for use in the preparation of the preliminary draft of the Treaty on the Denuclearization of Latin America as recommended in Commission resolution 10 (II),

Taking into account the fact that the working paper has been extremely useful both to Governments and to the Commission in performing their respective functions,

Decides to express its special gratitude to the Co-ordinating Committee for the invaluable contribution that the results of the work summarized in its report have made to the success of the Commission's third session.

(Adopted at the 33rd meeting, on 3 May 1966)

RESOLUTION 14 (III)

PROPOSALS FOR THE PREPARATION OF THE TREATY ON THE
DENUCLEARIZATION OF LATIN AMERICA

The Preparatory Commission for the Denuclearization of Latin America,

Having considered the working paper prepared by the Co-ordinating Committee and the draft Treaty submitted by the delegations of Brazil and Colombia, the parallel texts of which are reproduced in document COPREDAL/S/19/Rev.1, and the amendments and suggestions put forward by delegations, which are contained in document COPRE-DAL/S/20/Rev.2 and Add.1,

Decides

1. *To place on record* its especial gratitude to the Governments of Mexico and Chile for the observations (COPREDAL/CC/OAT/1 and Corr.1 and COPREDAL/CC/OAT/2) which they transmitted to the Co-ordinating Committee in accordance with resolution 9 (II), to the Governments of Brazil and Colombia for the draft Treaty referred to in the preceding paragraph, and to the Governments of all member States for the amendments and suggestions put

forward by their delegations, which have contributed so much to the success of the Commission's third session;

2. *To endorse* the document entitled "Proposals for the Preparation of the Treaty on the Denuclearization of Latin America" (COPRE-DAL/36), which is annexed to this resolution;

3. *To request* the General Secretary to transmit this document to the Governments of member States;

4. *To recommend* that the Governments should transmit to the General Secretary, as soon as possible, and in any event not later than 15 July 1966, any observations they see fit to make on this document, asking them to have such observations drafted preferably in the form of specific amendments to the relevant passages in the document;

5. *To instruct* the General Secretary to circulate the observations referred to in the previous paragraph to the Governments of Member States as he receives them;

6. *To request* the Chairman of the Commission to transmit the document in question to the Governments of the States with which the Negotiating Committee was in touch during the twentieth session of the United Nations General Assembly, asking them to inform him, if possible before 15 July 1966, of the attitude they intend to adopt, in the light of the contents of this document, towards the items which are relevant in each case from among the three mentioned in paragraph 6 (1) of the report of the Negotiating Committee (COPREDAL/CN/1).

7. *To request* the Chairman of the Commission to instruct the General Secretary to circulate the replies received from the Governments mentioned in the previous paragraph as he receives them, in the same way as is provided in paragraph 5 for the observations referred to therein.

ANNEX

PROPOSALS FOR THE PREPARATION OF THE TREATY ON THE
DENUCLEARIZATION OF LATIN AMERICA (COPREDAL/36)

(Adopted by the Preparatory Commission at its third session held from 19 April to 4 May 1966)

TREATY ON THE DENUCLEARIZATION
OF LATIN AMERICA
Preamble

In the name of their peoples and faithfully interpreting their desires and aspirations, the Governments represented at the Conference of Plenipotentiaries for the Denuclearization of Latin America,

Desiring to contribute, so far as lies in their power, towards ending the armaments race, especially in nuclear weapons, and towards strengthening a world at peace, based on the sovereign equality of States, mutual respect and good neighbourliness,

Recalling that the United Nations General Assembly, in its resolution 808 (IX), adopted unanimously as one of the three points of a co-ordinated programme of disarmament "the total prohibition of the use and manufacture of nuclear weapons and weapons of mass destruction of every type",

Recalling also United Nations General Assembly resolution 1911 (XVIII), which established that the measures that should be agreed upon for the denuclearization of Latin America should be taken "in the light of the principles of the Charter of the United Nations and of regional agreements",

Recalling that the Charter of the Organization of American States proclaims that it is an essential purpose of the organization to strengthen the peace and security of the continent,

Convinced:

That the incalculable destructive power of nuclear weapons has made it imperative that the legal prohibition of war should be strictly observed in practice if the survival of civilization and of mankind itself is to be assured;

That nuclear weapons, whose terrible effects are suffered, without distinction and without escape, by the armies and by the civilian population alike, constitute, through the persistence of the radioactivity they release, an attack on the integrity of the human species and ultimately may even render the whole Earth uninhabitable;

That general and complete disarmament under effective international control is a vital matter which all the peoples of the world equally demand;

That the proliferation of nuclear weapons, which seems inevitable unless States, in the exercise of their sovereign rights, use self-restraint in order to prevent it, would make any agreement on disarmament enormously difficult and would increase the danger of the outbreak of a nuclear conflagration;

That the establishment of denuclearized zones is closely linked with the maintenance of peace and security in the respective regions;

That the privileged situation of the States represented at the Conference, whose territories are wholly free from nuclear weapons, imposes upon them the inescapable duty of preserving that situation both in their own interests and for the good of mankind;

That the existence of nuclear weapons in any country of Latin America would make it a target for possible nuclear attacks and would inevitably set off, throughout the region, a ruinous race in nuclear weapons which would involve the unjustifiable diversion, for warlike purposes, of the limited resources available for economic and social development;

That the foregoing factors, coupled with the traditional peace-loving outlook of their peoples, make it essential that nuclear energy should be used in Latin America exclusively for peaceful purposes, giving the Latin American countries the greatest and most equitable possible access to the peaceful uses of the atom, in order to expedite the promotion of their development in all respects;

That the denuclearization of vast geographical areas, adopted by the sovereign decision of the States comprised therein, will exercise a beneficial influence on other regions, where similar conditions exist;

Convinced finally:

That the denuclearization of Latin America—being understood to mean the undertaking entered into internationally in this Treaty to keep their territories free for ever from nuclear weapons—will constitute a measure of protection for their peoples against the squandering of their limited resources on nuclear armaments and against possible nuclear attacks on their territories; a significant contribution towards preventing the proliferation of nuclear weapons and a powerful factor for general and complete disarmament; and

That Latin America, faithful to its tradition of universality, must not only endeavour to banish from its homelands the scourge of a nuclear war, but must also strive to promote the well-being and advancement of its peoples, at the same time co-operating in the fulfilment of the ideals of mankind, that is to say, in the consolidation of a lasting peace based on equal rights, economic fairness and social justice for all, in accordance with the principles and purposes of the Charter of the United Nations and with the nature, purposes and principles of the Organization of American States as set forth in its Charter,

Have agreed as follows:

Obligations

Article 1

1. The Contracting Parties hereby undertake to prohibit and prevent in their respective territories:

    (a) The testing, use, manufacture, production or acquisition by any means whatsoever of any nuclear weapons, by the Parties themselves, directly or indirectly, by anyone on their behalf or in any other way; and

(b) The receipt, storage installation, deployment and any form of possession of any nuclear weapon, directly or indirectly, by the Parties themselves, by anyone on their behalf or in any other way.

(b) The receipt, storage [transport], installation, deployment and any form of possession of any nuclear weapon, directly or indirectly, by the Parties themselves, by anyone on their behalf or in any other way.

2. The Contracting Parties also undertake to refrain from engaging in, encouraging or authorizing, directly or indirectly, or in any way participating in the testing, use, manufacture, production, possession of or control over any nuclear weapon.

Definition of "territory"

Article 2

For the purposes of this Treaty, the term "territory" shall be understood to include the territorial sea, air space and any other space over which the State has sovereignty under its own law.

Definition of "nuclear weapons"

Article 3

For the purposes of this Treaty, a "nuclear weapon" is defined as any device which is capable of releasing nuclear energy in an uncontrolled manner and is intended to be used for military purposes. Any instrument that may be used for the transport or propulsion of the device is not included in this definition if it is separable from the device and not an indivisible part thereof.

Organization

Article 4

1. In order to ensure fulfilment of the obligations of this Treaty, the Contracting Parties hereby establish an international organization to be known as the "Agency for the Denuclearization of Latin America", hereinafter referred to as "the Agency".
2. The Agency shall be responsible for the holding of periodic or extraordinary consultations among member States on matters relating to the purposes, measures and procedures set forth in this Treaty and supervision of compliance with the obligations arising therefrom.
3. The Contracting Parties agree to extend to the Agency full and prompt co-operation in accordance with the provisions of this

118

Treaty, of any agreements they may conclude with the Agency and of any agreements the Agency may conclude with any other international organization or body.

Organs

Article 5

1. There are hereby established as principal organs of the Agency a General Conference and a Secretariat.
2. Such subsidiary organs as are considered necessary may be established in accordance with this Treaty.

The General Conference

Article 6

1. The General Conference, the supreme organ of the Agency, shall be composed of all States [which are parties to this Treaty] and shall hold annual regular sessions [and special sessions whenever this Treaty so provides or the circumstances so require].

1. The General Conference, the supreme organ of the Agency, shall be composed of all [sovereign] States [situated south of the parallel of latitude 30 degrees north in the western hemisphere] and shall hold annual regular sessions [but may, nevertheless, hold special sessions whenever this Treaty so provides or the circumstances make this advisable].

2. The General Conference:

(a) May discuss any matter covered by this Treaty and take a decision thereon within the limits of the Treaty;

(b) Shall establish the procedures for the control system to ensure observance of this Treaty, in accordance with the provisions of the Treaty and its annexes;

(c) Shall elect the General Secretary;

(d) Shall receive and consider the annual and special reports submitted by the General Secretary;

(e) Together with the General Secretary, shall consider and initiate studies designed to facilitate the fulfilment of the aims of this Treaty;

(f) Shall be the organ competent to authorize the conclusion of agreements with Governments and other international organizations or bodies.

119

3. The General Conference shall adopt the Agency's budget and fix the scale of financial contributions to be made by member States, taking into account the systems and criteria used for the same purpose by the United Nations.

4. The General Conference shall elect its officers for each session and may establish such subsidiary organs as it deems necessary in order to discharge its functions.

5. The decisions of the General Conference shall be taken by the Parties present and voting, by a simple majority in the case of procedural matters and by a two-thirds majority in the case of matters relating to the control system, the measures referred to in article 15, the admission of new members, the election of the General Secretary and adoption of the budget. In other cases, it shall be decided by a simple majority whether a two-thirds majority is required.

6. The General Conference shall adopt its own rules of procedure.

Secretariat

A r t i c l e 7

1. The Secretariat shall consist of a General Secretary, who shall be the chief administrative official of the Agency, and of such staff as he requires. The General Secretary shall have a term of office of three years and may be re-elected.

2. The staff of the Secretariat shall be appointed by the General Secretary, in accordance with the instructions issued by the General Conference.

3. In addition to the functions assigned to him under this Treaty and to such others as may be assigned to him by the General Conference, the General Secretary shall ensure the proper operation of the control system established by this Treaty, in accordance with the provisions of the Treaty and the decisions taken by the General Conference.

4. The General Secretary shall act in that capacity at all sessions of the General Conference and shall make an annual report to it on the work of the Agency and any special reports that the General Conference may request of him or that he deems desirable.

5. The General Secretary shall establish the procedures for distribu-

ting, to all Contracting Parties, all information materials the Centre may receive from governmental or non-governmental sources.

6. In the performance of their duties, the General Secretary and the staff shall not seek or receive instructions from any Government or from any other authority external to the Agency and shall refrain from any action which might reflect on their position as international officials responsible only to the Agency; subject to their responsibility to the Agency, they shall not reveal any manufacturing secrets or any other confidential information that comes to their knowledge through the performance of their official duties in the Agency.

7. Each of the Contracting Parties undertakes to respect the exclusively international character of the responsibilities of the General Secretary and the staff and not to seek to influence them in the discharge of their responsibilities.

Control system

A r t i c l e   8

1. A control system is hereby established for the purpose of verifying fulfilment of the obligations arising out of this Treaty and, to that end, of verifying in particular:

[For the purpose of verifying fulfilment of the obligations entered into by the Contracting Parties in accordance with article 1, a control system shall be established and shall be put into effect in accordance with the provisions of articles 9-13 inclusive.]

(a) that devices, services and facilities intended for peaceful uses of nuclear energy are not used in the testing or manufacture of nuclear weapons;

(b) that none of the activities prohibited in article 1 of this Treaty are carried out in the territory of the Contracting Parties with nuclear materials or weapons introduced from abroad;

(c) that explosions for peaceful purposes are compatible with article 13 of this Treaty.

2. The procedures for putting into effect the control system referred to in paragraph 1 of this article are set forth in articles 9-13 of this Treaty.

A r t i c l e 9

The Contracting Parties [undertake to request the] International Atomic Energy Agency to apply [the] safeguards [of the Agency to special fissionable materials and] to nuclear facilities in their respective territories [and undertake to conclude the corresponding bilateral agreements. These safeguards agreements shall include all the provisions of the Safeguards System (1965) and The Agency's Inspectorate (GC (V) INF/39) that are applicable and such other provisions as are necessary in each case, including any amendments thereto made by the date of the agreement. These agreements shall enter into force, for each Party, not later than 180 days after the date of the deposit of its instrument of ratification of this Treaty].

The Contracting Parties [shall negotiate bilateral agreements with the] International Atomic Energy Agency [for] the application of [its] Safeguards [System] [approved by the ninth General Conference] to nuclear facilities [and activities] in their respective territories [including gaseous diffusion, centrifuge, chemical separation and reprocessing plants and any other plants for the production, refining or utilization of special fissionable material].

Reports of the Parties

A r t i c l e 10

1. The Contracting Parties shall submit to the Agency and to the International Atomic Energy Agency, for its information, semi-annual reports stating that no activity prohibited under this Treaty has occurred in their respective territories.

2. The Contracting Parties shall simultaneously transmit to the Agency a copy of any report relating to the matters which are the subject of this Treaty and to the application of the Safeguards which they may submit to the International Atomic Energy Agency.

3. The Contracting Parties shall also transmit to the Organization of

American States, for its information, any reports that may be of interest to it, in accordance with the obligations established by the Inter-American System.

Special reports requested by the General Secretary

A r t i c l e 11

1. The General Secretary may request any of the Contracting Parties to provide the Agency with complementary or supplementary information regarding any event or circumstance connected with the application of this Treaty, explaining his reasons. The Contracting Parties undertake to co-operate promptly and fully with the General Secretary.
2. The General Secretary shall inform all Contracting Parties forthwith of such requests and of the respective replies.

Special inspections

A r t i c l e 12

1. Special inspections may be carried out in the following circumstances:
   (a) By the International Atomic Energy Agency in accordance with the agreements referred to in article 9 of this Treaty;
   (b) If the General Secretary is so requested, the reasons for the request being stated, by any Party which suspects that some prohibited activity has been carried out, or is about to be carried out, in the territory of any other Contracting Party or anywhere on such latter Party's behalf;
   (c) If the General Secretary is so requested by any Party which is suspected or accused of having violated the Treaty. The General Secretary shall arrange immediately for such an inspection to be carried out.
2. The costs and expenses of any special inspection carried out under paragraph 1, sub-paragraph (b) or (c), of this article shall be borne by the requesting Party or Parties, except where the report on the special inspection concludes that, in view of the relevant circumstances, such costs and expenses should be borne by the Agency.
3. The General Conference shall formulate the procedures for the organization and execution of any special inspections that may be carried out in accordance with paragraph 1, sub-paragraphs (b) and (c), of this article.

4. The Contracting Parties shall undertake to grant the inspectors carrying out such special inspections full and free access to whatever places and information may be necessary for the performance of their duties. If so requested by the authorities of the Contracting Party in whose territory the inspection is carried out, the inspectors appointed by the Conference shall be accompanied by representatives of the said authorities, provided that this does not in any way delay or hinder the work of the inspectors.

5. The General Secretary shall immediately transmit to all the Contracting Parties a copy of the report pursuant to any special inspection.

6. Similarly, the General Secretary shall immediately send to the Secretary-General of the United Nations, for the information of the Security Council and the General Assembly, a copy of any report pursuant to any special inspection.

7. The General Secretary, or any of the Contracting Parties, may request a special session of the Conference for the purpose of considering the report pursuant to any special inspection. The General Secretary shall convene a special session of the General Conference when so requested by any Contracting Party.

8. The General Conference, convened in special session under this article, may make recommendations to the Contracting Parties and submit reports to the Secretary-General of the United Nations for the information of the Security Council and the General Assembly.

Explosions for peaceful purposes

A r t i c l e 13

1. The Contracting Parties may carry out explosions of nuclear devices for peaceful purposes—including explosions which involve devices similar to those used in nuclear weapons—or assist third parties, or be assisted by third parties, for the same purpose, provided that they do so in accordance with the provisions of this article.

2. Parties intending to carry out, or co-operate in the carrying out of, such an explosion shall notify the Agency, as far in advance as the circumstances require, of the date of the explosion and shall at the same time provide the following information:

(a) The nature of the nuclear device and the source from which it was obtained;

(b) The date, place and purpose of the proposed explosion;

(c) The procedures which will be followed in order to comply with paragraph 3 of this article;

(d) The expected force of the device;

(e) The fullest possible information on any radioactive fall-out that may result from the explosion or explosions, and the measures which will be taken to avoid danger to the population and territories of any other Party or Parties.

3. Members of the Secretariat and of the staff of the International Atomic Energy Agency may observe all the preparations, including the explosion of the device, and shall have unrestricted access to any area in the vicinity of the explosion, in order to ascertain whether the device and the procedures followed during the explosion are in conformity with the information submitted in accordance with paragraph 2 of the present article.

Relations with other international organizations

A r t i c l e 14

1. The Agency may conclude such agreements with the International Atomic Energy Agency as it considers likely to facilitate the efficient operation of the control system established by this Treaty.

2. The Agency may also enter into relations with any international organization or body, especially any which may be established in the future to supervise disarmament or measures for the control of armaments in any part of the world.

3. The Contracting Parties may, if they see fit, request the advice of the Inter-American Nuclear Energy Commission on all technical matters connected with the application of the Treaty with which the Commission is competent to deal under its statutes.

Measures in the event of violation of the Treaty

A r t i c l e 15

1. The General Conference shall take note of all cases in which, in its opinion, any Contracting Party is not complying fully with its obligations under this Treaty and shall draw the matter to the attention of the Party concerned, making such recommendations as it deems appropriate.

2. If, in its opinion, such non-compliance constitutes a violation of the Treaty which might endanger peace and security, the General Conference shall report thereon simultaneously to the Security Council and the General Assembly through the Secretary-General of the United Nations and to the Council of the Organization of American States. The General Conference shall likewise report to the International Atomic Energy Agency for such purposes as are relevant in accordance with its Statutes.

A r t i c l e 16

None of the provisions of this Treaty shall be construed as impairing the rights and obligations of the Parties under the Charter of the United Nations or, in the case of States members of the Organization of American States, under existing regional treaties.

Prerogatives and immunities

A r t i c l e 17

1. The Agency shall enjoy in the territory of each of the Contracting Parties such prerogatives and immunities as are necessary for the exercise of its functions and may conclude agreements with the Contracting Parties to this end.
2. Representatives of the Contracting Parties accredited to the Agency and members of its staff shall also enjoy such prerogatives and immunities as are necessary for the performance of their duties.

Notification of other agreements

A r t i c l e 18

Once this Treaty has entered into force, the Secretariat shall be notified immediately of any international agreement concluded by any of the Contracting Parties on matters with which this Treaty is concerned; the Secretariat shall register it and notify the other Contracting Parties.

Settlement of disputes

A r t i c l e 19

1. Unless the Parties concerned agree on another mode of peaceful settlement, any question or dispute concerning the interpretation or application of this Treaty which is not settled shall be referred to the International Court of Justice, subject to the consent of the Parties.
2. The General Conference shall be empowered, subject to authorization from the General Assembly of the United Nations, to request the International Court of Justice to give an opinion on any legal question arising within the scope of the Agency's activities.

A r t i c l e 20

1. This Treaty shall be open for signature [or accession to:

    (a) All Latin American republics;

    (b) The other present and future sovereign States of the western hemisphere situated in their entirety south of latitude 30° North, which express their desire to accede to this Treaty and are admitted by the General Conference;

    (c) States inside or outside the continent which have, *de jure* or *de facto,* international responsibility for territories situated in the western hemisphere south of latitude 30° North, with reference to the territories in respect of which they agree to accept the obligations arising out of this Treaty].

2. Nothing in this article shall be construed as prejudging the status of the territories [referred to in paragraph 1 (c)].

1. This Treaty shall be open for signature [and accession to all Latin American States. It shall also be open to other present and future sovereign States which are situated in the western hemisphere south of latitude 30° North, except as provided in paragraph 3 of this article].

2. Nothing in this article shall be construed as prejudging the status of the territories [situated in the western hemisphere south of latitude 30° North, for which States inside or outside the continent have, *de jure* or *de facto,* international responsibility].

3. The General Conference shall not take any decision regarding the admission of a political entity whose territory is, in whole or in part and prior to the date of signature of this Treaty, the subject of a dispute or claim between a country outside the continent and one or more Latin American States until the dispute has been settled by peaceful means.

Ratification and deposit

A r t i c l e 21

1. This Treaty shall be subject to ratification or accession by signatory States in accordance with their respective constitutional procedures.
2. The Treaty and the instruments of ratification or accession shall be deposited with the Government of ...., which is hereby designated the Depositary Government.
3. The Depositary Government shall send certified copies of the Treaty to the Governments of signatory and acceding States and shall notify them of the deposit of each instrument of ratification or accession.

Reservations

A r t i c l e 22

This Treaty shall not be subject to reservations.

Entry into force

A r t i c l e 23

1. The Treaty shall enter into force [between the States which have ratified it or acceded to it on the date on which they deposit their respective instruments of ratification or accession].
[2. The Agency shall start to operate when eleven instruments of ratification or accession have been deposited.]

1. [This] Treaty shall enter into force [as soon as the following requirements have been complied with:]

(a) Transmittal to the Depositary Government of the instruments of ratification of this Treaty by the Governments of the States mentioned in article 20, except as provided in paragraph 3 of that article.

(b) Signature and ratification of the Additional Protocol of Guarantee I, annex I to this Treaty, by all the "nuclear Powers";

(c) Signature and ratification of the Additional Protocol

of Guarantee II, annex II to this Treaty, by the Governments of all States which have, *de jure* or *de facto*, international responsibility for territories situated in the western hemisphere south of latitude 30° North;

(d) Conclusion of bilateral agreements on the application of the Safeguards System of the International Atomic Energy Agency, in accordance with article 9 of this Treaty.

2. "Nuclear Powers" shall be understood to mean those States which possess, under their exclusive national control, the nuclear weapons defined in article 3 of this Treaty.]

NOTE: The working paper of the Co-ordinating Committee contained no specific provisions concerning the obtaining of guarantees from the nuclear Powers because this aspect was already covered in the report of the Negotiating Committee, which put forward a specific procedure to be followed in this matter and an outline draft resolution to be submitted in due course to the General Assembly of the United Nations (annex 1).

NOTE: The draft Treaty submitted by the delegations of Brazil and Colombia included in addition to the provisions contained in this article, two draft Additional Protocols of Guarantee (annex 2).

Amendments

Article 24

1. Any Contracting Party may propose amendments to this Treaty, through the General Secretary of the Agency, who shall transmit them to all the other Contracting Parties. The General Secretary shall immediately convene a special session of the General Conference to consider such proposals, for the adoption of which a two-thirds majority of the Contracting Parties present and voting shall be required.

2. Amendments adopted shall enter into force as soon as the requirements set forth in article 23 of this Treaty have been complied with.

Duration and denunciation

A r t i c l e 25

1. This Treaty shall be of a permanent nature and shall remain in force indefinitely, but any Party may denounce it by notifying the General Secretary of the Agency if, in the opinion of the denouncing State, there have arisen or may arise circumstances connected with the content of the Treaty which affect its supreme interests and the peace and security of one or more Contracting Parties.

(New paragraph)

2. This Treaty may also be denounced in the following cases:
    (a) By unilateral decision of any of the Contracting Parties because of the violation or denunciation of one or more provisions of the Additional Protocol of Guarantee I, annex I to this Treaty;
    (b) By unilateral decision of any of the Contracting Parties because of the violation or denunciation of one or more provisions of the Additional Protocol of Guarantee II, annex II to this Treaty;
    (c) By unilateral decision of any of the Contracting Parties, if any State that becomes a "nuclear Power" does not, for any reason, sign the Additional Protocol of Guarantee I, annex I to this Treaty, within a period of not more than 180 days from the date on which its status as a "nuclear Power" is made public.

3. The denunciation shall take effect three months after the General Secretary of the Agency is notified by the Government of the signatory State concerned. The General Secretary shall immediately communicate such notification to the other Contracting Parties and to the Secretary-General of the United Nations for the information of the Security Council and the General Assembly. He shall also communicate it to the Secretary General of the Organization of American States.

Authentic texts and registration

A r t i c l e 26

This Treaty, of which the Chinese, English, French, Portuguese, Russian and Spanish texts are equally authentic, shall be registered by the Depositary Government in accordance with Article 102 of the Charter of the United Nations. The Depositary Government shall notify the Secretary-General of the United Nations of the signatures, ratifications, accessions and amendments relating to this Treaty and shall communicate them to the Secretary General of the Organization of American States for his information.

In witness whereof the undersigned Plenipotentiaries, having deposited their full powers, found in good and due form, sign this Treaty on behalf of their respective Governments.

Done at ... , on the ... days of the month of ... 19 ....

ANNEX 1 *

PARAGRAPHS 7 AND 8 OF THE REPORT OF THE NEGOTIATING COMMITTEE (COPREDAL/CN/1), WHICH CONTAIN THE COMMITTEE'S SUGGESTIONS REGARDING THE PROCEDURE WHEREBY THE NUCLEAR POWERS MAY APPROPRIATELY UNDERTAKE TO RESPECT THE LEGAL STATUS OF THE DENUCLEARIZATION OF LATIN AMERICA, INCLUDING THE OUTLINE DRAFT RESOLUTION PREPARED BY THE COMMITTEE FOR SUBMISSION TO THE GENERAL ASSEMBLY OF THE UNITED STATES

7. The members of the Negotiating Committee next considered what specific procedure could be suggested for the consideration of the nuclear Powers whereby they might appropriately enter into the commitment referred to in resolution 1 (I) of the Preparatory Commission, namely, to respect the legal instrument of the denuclearization of Latin America, and came to the conclusion that a suitable method of achieving the desired end might be the following:

(1) Once the Treaty on the Denuclearization of Latin America had been signed, its text would be sent to the Secretary-General of the United Nations for circulation as a document of the General Assembly of that Organization in connexion with its resolution 1911 (XVIII).

(2) At the session of the General Assembly immediately following signature of the Treaty, the signatory States would request the inclusion in the Assembly's agenda of an item entitled "Treaty on the denuclearization of Latin America".

(3) The signatory States (or a group of them), together with any other States Members of the United Nations that so desired, would submit to the Committee of the Assembly responsible for dealing with the item a draft resolution which, among such other provisions as might be considered appropriate, would contain two whereby the Committee would:

(a) Recognize that, in order that the Treaty on the Denuclearization of Latin America should be as effective as possible, it was highly advisable that all States, and particularly the nuclear States, should undertake to refrain from taking, directly or

* See note to article 23, left-hand column, page 129.

indirectly, for whatever reason, any action that might jeopardize faithful compliance with the provisions of the Treaty;

(b) Declare that any State voting in favour of the resolution or subsequently acceding to it would automatically be assuming the commitment referred to in the preceding paragraph.

8. This procedure, apart from its simplicity and the ease with which it could be put into effect, would have the advantage of making it possible, not just for the nuclear Powers, but for all other States in the world, whether or not they are at present members of the United Nations, automatically to assume the commitment in question at any time they so desired.

Outline of a possible draft resolution of the General Assembly of the United Nations, submitted by the Negotiating Committee to the representatives of the nuclear States for consideration by their respective Governments

The General Assembly,

Having considered the Treaty on the Denuclearization of Latin America (A/ . . .), the text of which was transmitted to it by the signatory States,

(Here would follow any other preambular paragraphs that might be considered appropriate.)

1. *Expresses* its particular appreciation of the methodical and assiduous work done by the Signatory States, which has led to the conclusion of the Treaty on the Denuclearization of Latin America, this Treaty being an important contribution towards preventing the proliferation of nuclear weapons;

(Here would follow any other paragraphs that might be thought appropriate to insert before the last two, which would be worded as follows.)

X. *Recognizes* that, in order to ensure that the Treaty on the Denuclearization of Latin America is as effective as possible, it is highly advisable that all States, and particularly the nuclear States, should undertake to refrain from taking, directly or indirectly, for whatever reason, any action that might jeopardize faithful compliance with the provisions of the Treaty;

XX. *Declares* that any State which votes in favour of this resolution or subsequently accedes to it will be automatically assuming the commitment referred to in the preceding paragraph.

ANNEX 2 *

I / Protocol of Guarantee

The undersigned Plenipotentiaries, being vested with full powers, respectively, by the President of the United States of America; the President of the French Republic; Her Majesty the Queen of the United Kingdom and of Her other Realms and Territories, Queen, Head of the Commonwealth; the Chairman of the Presidium of the Union of Soviet Socialist Republics; and the President of the People's Republic of China.

Convinced that the Multilateral Treaty on the Denuclearization of Latin America, negotiated and signed pursuant to the recommendations of the General Assembly of the United Nations contained in resolution 1911 (XVIII) of 27 November 1963, is an important step forward towards ensuring the non-proliferation of nuclear weapons,

Conscious that the non-proliferation of nuclear weapons is not an end in itself but a means of achieving general and complete disarmament at a later stage,

Desiring to contribute, so far as lies in their power, towards ending the arms race, particularly in the field of nuclear weapons, and towards promoting and strengthening peace in the world, based on mutual respect and the sovereign equality of States,

Have agreed as follows:

Article 1. The status of denuclearization of Latin America as defined, delimited and formulated in the provisions of the Multilateral Treaty to which this Protocol is annexed shall be fully respected by the signatories of the present instrument as regards all its express aims and provisions.

Article 2. The Governments represented by the undersigned Plenipotentiaries accordingly undertake not to contribute in any way to the performance of the following acts in the territory defined in the aforesaid Treaty:

(a) The testing, use, manufacture, production or acquisition by any means whatsoever of nuclear weapons, either directly or by anyone on behalf of others;

(b) The receipt, storage or installation of any nuclear weapon or launching device, either directly or by anyone on behalf of others.

Article 3. The Governments represented by the undersigned Pleni-

---

* See note to article 23, right-hand column, page 129.

potentiaries also undertake to give the Contracting Parties to the Multilateral Treaty to which this Protocol is annexed, while it remains in force, full guarantees that they will not take the initiative in the use of nuclear weapons, of any kind, against any part of the territory included in the area defined in the aforesaid Treaty, provided that this same commitment is assumed by all other Powers possessing nuclear weapons.

Article 4. This Protocol shall have the same duration as the Multilateral Treaty on the Denuclearization of Latin America to which it is annexed, and the provisions concerning ratification and denunciation appearing in the body of the Treaty shall apply to it.

In witness whereof, the undersigned Plenipotentiaries, having deposited their full powers, found in good and due form, have signed this Protocol of Guarantee on behalf of their respective Governments.

Done at . . . , in the Chinese, English, French, Portuguese, Russian and Spanish languages, on the ... days of the month of ... 19 ... .

II / Protocol of Guarantee

The undersigned Plenipotentiaries, being vested with full powers, respectively, by the President of the United States of America; the President of the French Republic; Her Majesty the Queen of the United Kingdom and of Her other Realms and Territories, Queen, Head of the Commonwealth; and Her Majesty the Queen of the Netherlands,

Convinced that the Multilateral Treaty on the Denuclearization of Latin America negotiated and signed pursuant to the recommendations of the General Assembly of the United Nations contained in resolution 1911 (XVIII) of 27 November 1963, is an important step forward towards ensuring the non-proliferation of nuclear weapons,

Conscious that the non-proliferation of nuclear weapons is not an end in itself, but a means of achieving general and complete disarmament at a later stage,

Desiring to contribute, so far as lies in their power towards ending the arms race, particularly in the field of nuclear weapons, and towards promoting the strengthening of peace in the world, based on mutual respect and the sovereign equality of States,

Have agreed as follows:

Article 1. The status of denuclearization of Latin America, as defined, delimited and formulated in the provisions of the Multilateral Treaty to which this Protocol is annexed, shall be fully respected by the above-mentioned signatory Governments as regards all its express aims and provisions, with respect to the territories for which they have, *de jure* or *de facto*, international responsibility and which lie within the geographical area to which the Treaty applies.

Article 2. This Protocol shall have the same duration as the Multilateral Treaty on the denuclearization of Latin America to which it is annexed and the provisions concerning ratification and denunciation appearing in the body of the Treaty shall apply to it.

In witness whereof, the undersigned Plenipotentiaries, having deposited their full powers, found in good and due form, have signed this Protocol of Guarantee on behalf of their respective Governments.

Done at . . . , in the Chinese, English, French, Portuguese, Russian and Spanish languages, on the . . . days of the month of . . . 19 . . . .

(Adopted at the 33rd meeting on 3 May 1966)

RESOLUTION 15 (III)

AMENDMENTS SUBMITTED BY THE DELEGATION OF VENEZUELA

The Preparatory Commission for the Denuclearization of Latin America,

Considering the fact that the amendments submitted by the delegation of Venezuela in document COPREDAL/L/14 could not be examined at the third session with the attention and care that their importance warrant,

Decides

To request the General Secretary to transmit copies of the said document to the Governments of member States, inviting them to take these amendments into account when considering the text of the proposals for the drafting of the Treaty on the Denuclearization of Latin America adopted by the Commission in resolution 14 (III).

(Adopted at the 33rd meeting on 3 May 1966)

RESOLUTION 16 (III)

FOURTH SESSION OF THE PREPARATORY COMMISSION

The Preparatory Commission for the Denuclearization of Latin America,

Recalling resolution 1911 (XVIII), adopted by the General Assembly of the United Nations on 27 November 1963,

Recalling also its resolution 10 (II), adopted on 31 August 1965,

Noting that the results of its discussions at its third session and the content of the proposals for the drafting of the Treaty on the Denuclearization of Latin America adopted in its resolution 14 (III) indicate that further efforts must be made jointly, before the twenty-first session of the United Nations General Assembly, to eliminate the differences of opinion that still exist on some aspects of the Treaty's contents,

Decides

1. To set Tuesday, 30 August 1966, as the date of the first meeting of the fourth session of the Preparatory Commission for the Denuclearization of Latin America;

2. *To call upon* the Governments of member States to make special efforts and to take all measures they deem appropriate in order to help to reach a concensus on the points of difference that still exist.

(Adopted at the 33rd meeting, on 3 May 1966)

RESOLUTION 17 (III)

APPEAL TO THE NUCLEAR POWERS

The Preparatory Commission for the Denuclearization of Latin America,

Noting that tests of nuclear weapons constitute a form of proliferation of such weapons, and convinced that it is necessary to put an end to their proliferation,

Determined to ensure that the territory of Latin America remains free from the lethal effects of nuclear weapons,

Being informed that new nuclear weapon tests are shortly to be held which may endanger and harm the health of the inhabitants of some regions of Latin America, the maritime resources and other sources of production in the sea itself or in contiguous American waters and coasts, and have other unforeseeable and incalculable repercussions,

Recalling that the General Assembly of the United Nations, in resolution 1762 (XVII), expressly condemned "all nuclear weapon tests" without exception,

Expressing its concern at the fact that so far the nuclear Powers have not been able to reach agreement on the cessation of nuclear weapon tests in all environments,

Decides

1. *To address a solemn appeal* to the nuclear Powers to cease nuclear weapon tests of all kinds;

2. *To express the hope* that new nuclear tests which might endanger the health of the peoples of Latin America or harm its maritime and other natural resources will not be conducted.

(Adopted at the 34th meeting, on 4 May 1966)

RESOLUTION 18 (III)

The Preparatory Commission for the Denuclearization of Latin America,

Bearing in mind the policy followed by Mr. Gustavo Diaz Ordaz, President of the United Mexican States, in supporting without reservation the development of the peaceful uses of nuclear energy while at the same time steadfastly striving to bring about a permanent ban on atomic weapons in Latin America,

Having received with deep appreciation the message which the President of the Mexican Republic personally addressed to it at the opening of its third plenary session,

Considering the interest which, in accordance with the above-mentioned policy, the Mexican Government has always shown in the proposal to denuclearize this geographical region and which has been reflected in the excellent facilities provided for the Preparatory Commission,

Decides

1. *To express* to Mr. Gustavo Díaz Ordaz, President of the United Mexican States, and to Mr. Antonio Carrillo Flores, Minister for Foreign Affairs of Mexico, its deep gratitude for the facilities with which their Government has provided to the Preparatory Commission during its third session, including the use, for the first time, of the magnificent conference area in the new building of the Mexican Ministry of Foreign Affairs;

2. *To congratulate* once more Ambassador Alfonso García Robles, Chairman of the Commission, on the results of the proceedings over which he presided;

3. *To convey* to Mr. Carlos Peón del Valle, General Secretary of the Commission, Mr. Antonio González de León, Deputy Secretary, and Mr. Manuel Tello Macías and Mr. Sergio González Galvez, who acted as secretaries of the Working Groups, an expression of well deserved thanks for the services they and their efficient colleagues have provided.

(Adopted at the 34th meeting, on 4 May 1966)

This Final Act was adopted unanimously by the Preparatory Commission for the Denuclearization of Latin America at the closing meeting of its third session, held on Wednesday, 4 May 1966.

19 Note Addressed to the Chairman of the Preparatory Commission by the French Ambassador to Mexico ▪ Headquarters of the Commission ▪ on 26 July 1966[7]

Mexico, D.F., 26 July 1966

No. 515

Dear Mr. Chairman:

In your letter of 6 May 1966, you kindly transmitted to me the Final Act of the Third Session of the Preparatory Commission for the Denuclearization of Latin America and you requested that I inform you what attitude my Government would adopt, in such an event, with regard to the statute which the Member countries of the Commission propose to prepare for all the territories of the region concerned.

The French Government, which, as you know, follows with sympathy the efforts of the Latin American countries, has carefully studied the texts that I transmitted to it. However, inasmuch as my Government is not participating in the negotiations, it will not be able to give its views in full knowledge of the facts until the Members of the Commission have successfully completed their work.

You may, nevertheless, be sure that this does not mean that France views any less favorably an attempt to limit the spread of nuclear arms voluntarily undertaken by the interested countries. It is in this context that the French Government would be able to state its intention of not taking any action with regard to the Latin American States that would

[7] Doc. COPREDAL/47. Unofficial translation.

140

encourage in their territories the development of nuclear activities of a military nature.

Concerning our departments in America, I wish to remind you that France has no intention of carrying out nuclear experiments in them and, in particular, that the activities of the Space Center of Guiana relate only to tests of special rockets and the launching of satellites.

These, Mr. Chairman, are the observations that I am able to furnish you. I should like to add that my Government has appreciated the spirit in which the deliberations of Mexico are being carried out and is pleased to note the great interest shown under your presidency by the distinguished representatives of the Latin American Republics and that, moved by the sentiments of friendship that we feel for them, it will follow with attention the continuation of their work.

I avail myself of this opportunity to renew to your Excellency the assurances of my highest consideration.

(SIGNED) Jacques Vimont

His Excellency, Ambassador Alfonso García Robles,
Chairman of the Preparatory Commission for the Denuclearization of Latin America,
Mexico City.

20 Note Addressed to the Chairman of the Preparatory Commission by the British Ambassador to Mexico ▪ Headquarters of the Commission ▪ on 24 August 1966

(1193/1)   24 August, 1966.

Your Excellency,

I have the honour to convey to you herewith the reply of my Government to the request of the Preparatory Commission for the Denuclearization of Latin America, contained in Your Excellency's note COPREDAL/44 of the 6th of May, 1966, and re-affirmed in the resolution of the Co-ordinating Committee at its session of the 15th of August.

I have the honour to request that my Government's comments on the questions referred to it be communicated to the Members of the Preparatory Commission.

I avail myself of this opportunity to renew to Your Excellency the assurances of my highest consideration.

(N. J. A. Cheetham)

His Excellency Sr. Lic. Alfonso García Robles,
Chairman of the Preparatory Commission for the Denuclearization of Latin America,
Ministry of Foreign Affairs, Mexico, D.F.

Her Majesty's Government have the honour to refer to paragraphs 4 and 6 of Resolution 14 (III) of the Preparatory Commission for the Denuclearisation of Latin America and welcome this opportunity, through the kind offices of the General Secretary, to inform the Governments of Member States of certain observations by Her Majesty's Government on the Proposals for the Preparation of the Treaty on the Denuclearisation of Latin America (COPREDAL/38) which were adopted by the Preparatory Commission at its third session from 19 April to 4 May, 1966.

Article 2

The Comments on Article 2 of the Working Document submitted by the Co-ordinating Committee to the Preparatory Commission (COPREDAL/CC/DT/1) stated that the definition chosen by the drafters was intended to include the continental shelf in the area to be covered by the treaty. Her Majesty's Government would wish to point out that the Geneva Convention on the Continental Shelf, of which the United Kingdom is a signatory, together with fourteen Latin American states, does not grant the coastal state sovereignty over the continental shelf adjacent to its coast and confirms the status of the super-adjacent waters as high seas. Her Majesty's Government would find difficulty in agreeing to a treaty which was inconsistent with these provisions of the Geneva Convention, and venture to express the hope that complex legal questions of this sort which are, by their nature, not related to the question of denuclearisation will not be allowed to prejudice the aims of the treaty.

Article 3

Her Majesty's Government are pleased to see that the draft originally proposed by Working Group B has been amended so as to remove any difficulties which might have arisen from the inclusion, in the definition of nuclear weapons, of modern ships and aircraft capable of use in a nuclear role although not actually carrying nuclear arms.

Her Majesty's Government understand that the inclusion of the phrase "in an uncontrolled manner" *inter alia* would permit the deployment in the Treaty area of vessels propelled by nuclear power for military as well as for civil purposes. In Her Majesty's Government's view, these could not come within the meaning of the term "device" by virtue alone of their method of propulsion.

Article 8

Paragraph 1 (c): Her Majesty's Government wish to express certain doubts about the desirability of Article 13 and these are set out below.

Article 9

Her Majesty's Government trust that there will be full consultation between the Preparatory Commission and the Governors of the International Atomic Energy Agency before the final form of this Article is drafted, to ensure that the facilities available to the International Atomic Energy Agency for the application of safeguards are adequate for the purposes intended.

Article 10

Paragraph 3. Her Majesty's Government are not a member of the Organisation of American States and would be unable to accept obligations in respect of the inter-American system even if they became full contracting parties to a Treaty with equal status with all other contracting parties. Her Majesty's Government venture to propose, therefore, that Paragraph 3 of the Article should simply read "the contracting parties shall also transmit to the Organisation of American States, for its information, any reports that may be of interest to it."

Article 12

It is understood that, in the selection of inspectors for action under this Article, care would be taken not to select persons who, for personal or nationality reasons or reasons unconnected with their functions, might be unsuitable for service in a given country; for example, a person convicted of serious crime or who had shown political hostility to a given country would hardly be regarded as suitable.

Article 13

Studies made by Her Majesty's Government on the subject of the use of nuclear explosions for peaceful purposes have shown that it is difficult, if not impossible, effectively to draw a distinction between a device for these purposes and a military weapon. A State having effective access to any sort of nuclear explosive device and also having the means to deliver it would have a readily usable military nuclear capability. The acquisition by a non-nuclear power of such a capability would not conform with the generally expressed desire to avoid the proliferation of nuclear arms. Moreover, the Partial Test Ban Treaty of 1963 would be contravened by a peaceful nuclear explosion unless it were entirely contained underground or unless the fission products created by it were entirely confined within the national boundaries of the State conducting the explosion: it would be most difficult to guarantee these conditions without possessing very advanced knowledge of nuclear explosions. Her Majesty's Government would most earnestly regret any form of proliferation of nuclear arms and feel obliged to express the gravest doubts about the inclusion in the Treaty of an Article in these terms.

Her Majesty's Government similarly believe that the granting of unrestricted access to the area of a peaceful nuclear explosion by members of the Secretariat or of the staff of the International Atomic Energy Agency who are not themselves nationals of countries already possessing nuclear weapons would be bound to result in the dissemination of nuclear weapon technology.

Article 20

Her Majesty's Government have consulted the Administrations of all British dependent territories within the proposed area indicated in this Article. None of these has any objection to their inclusion in a Treaty provided that its provisions are otherwise acceptable.

Paragraph 1 (b): Since the continent and islands of Antarctica are already the subject of an agreement not to introduce nuclear arms into the region, the risk of any conflict between similar agreements covering the same territory could be excluded by restricting the Latin American zone to the continental mainland and adjacent islands. This could be achieved by imposing a southern limit to the proposed zone at 60°S where the Antarctic Treaty begins.

Paragraph 3: It appears desirable that most, if not all, territories in the region, should they agree, form part of a nuclear-free zone; but this paragraph would appear to provoke political controversy and the raising of unrelated questions. It might also give rise to difficulties in connexion with certain areas and thus prejudice the success of the treaty as a whole. Her Majesty's Government would therefore prefer the exclusion of paragraph 3. It is not clear from either of the alternative drafts of paragraphs 1 and 2 of this Article in precisely what way Her Majesty's Government would be associated with the Treaty on behalf of dependent territories within the treaty area. Indeed, the second alternative does not seem to apply to any extra-continental State having dependent territories in the area, since they might not normally be described as "sovereign States which are situated, etc.". Her Majesty's Government would be grateful if any re-draft of the Article would make it clear that extra-continental powers, having dependencies in the area, would be invited to become contracting parties on behalf of these dependencies and would also be grateful if provision were made enabling such of these territories as become sovereign to accede in their own right in due course.

Article 23

Her Majesty's Government have frequently stated, as one of their basic principles for the creation of nuclear-free zones, that such zones should comprise all militarily significant states, and preferably all states, in the area in question. But this is not a rigid position and Her Majesty's Government would have to decide their attitude towards any partial zone according to circumstances: they would not exclude the possibility of giving support to a restricted zone which excluded some states, even militarily significant ones, if such a restricted zone would have a reasonable prospect of existing as a viable entity and particularly if it appeared likely to form a reasonable foundation on which a comprehensive zone could be built.

The note on the first alternative however refers to the obtaining of guarantees from the nuclear powers through a resolution in the United Nations General Assembly. This appears to Her Majesty's Government to present difficulties since General Assembly resolutions (with one or two exceptions which are not relevant here) have no mandatory effect and cannot therefore impose contractual obligations on those who vote for them. Her Majesty's Government therefore have doubts about the legal possibility of this course of action and about whether it is desirable to create in the United Nations a precedent of this character. The alternative method of seeking guarantees from the nuclear powers by inviting them to sign and ratify an appropriate additional Protocol is, therefore, to be preferred from the legal point of view.

Articles 24 and 25

These Articles would present no difficulties if Her Majesty's Government become a Contracting Party to the Treaty under the first alternative draft of Article 23.

FIRST PROTOCOL OF GUARANTEES

Article 2 sub-paragraph (b)

To bring the Protocol into line with the provisions of the Treaty itself, the words "or launching device" should be omitted.

21 Note Addressed to the Chairman of the Preparatory Commission by the United States Ambassador to Mexico ▪ Headquarters of the Commission ▪ on 29 August 1966

México, D. F., August 29, 1966.

Dear Mr. President:

Pursuant to your request of May 6, 1966, I am pleased to transmit herewith the official comments of the United States Government on the "Draft Proposals for Drafting the Latin American Denuclearization Treaty."

The United States has followed with interest the efforts to achieve a Nuclear-Free Zone in Latin America, and we welcome the effort and would be glad to see it reach a successful conclusion. Such success would constitute an excellent example of Latin American leadership and would strengthen world peace by helping to prevent the spread of nuclear weapons while maintaining hemispheric security. The United States has thus given careful attention to the draft proposals, and we hope that the following comments will prove of value in the deliberations of the Preparatory Commission.

Article 1

1. The United States believes that Articles 1, 3, 8, and 13 should be changed so as to prohibit the development of all nuclear explo-

sives, whatever their intended use. In particular, the United States believes that the obligations in Article 1 should be stated to apply to "nuclear weapons or other nuclear explosives," except that the treaty should permit the contracting parties to request states which possess nuclear explosive devices to perform detonations for peaceful purposes under appropriate procedures. This could be accomplished by making suitable changes in Article 13, and by inserting in Article 1 the phrase, "except as provided in Article 13."

2. The United States assumes that the proposed treaty would impose no prohibition that would restrict the freedom of transit within the western hemisphere. The US policy on freedom of transit is based on our national security needs and the vital security interests of the hemisphere, and we do not believe a Nuclear-Free Zone need, or should compromise this freedom. We therefore assume that the language of Article 1 as finally agreed will not in any way impair the freedom of transit now enjoyed by all powers.

Article 2

We suggest the deletion of the language "in accordance with its own legislation" (de acuerdo con su propia legislacion). This language raises serious problems of territorial sovereignty which cannot realistically be resolved in the context of a Nuclear-Free Zone Treaty and would have to be dealt with elsewhere.

Article 3

We recommend that this article be changed to reflect our other remarks concerning "peaceful purposes" explosions.

Article 8

We recommend that this article be changed to reflect our other remarks concerning "peaceful purposes" explosions.

Article 13

We agree that Article 13 should permit the contracting parties to arrange with nuclear powers for nuclear explosions for peaceful purposes, but believe that it should not provide for the acquisition or development by the contracting parties of their own nuclear devices for such purposes. We recommend that Article 13 specifically prohibit the testing, manufacture, or other acquisition of all nuclear explosives by the contracting parties.

The development of any nuclear explosive device by such a party, even if intended for a non-military purpose, would be essentially indistinguishable from a weapons development program and would necessarily provide information directly pertinent for such a program. The effect on triggering further nuclear proliferation by neighbors and potential adversaries would be virtually the same as from building a bomb. This is particularly so, since any nuclear explosive intended for peaceful applications could be used as a weapon, or could be readily adapted for such use. If a Nuclear-Free Zone Treaty, therefore, permitted the manufacture or acquisition without appropriate controls of nuclear explosive devices for peaceful purposes, the treaty would be rendered virtually meaningless.

The United States believes, however, that possible future benefits of peaceful nuclear explosions should be made available to all states, whether or not they possess nuclear weapons, but in a manner which would not contribute in any way to nuclear proliferation. Accordingly, the United States believes that if and when peaceful applications of nuclear explosives that are permissible under test ban treaty limitations prove technically and economically feasible, states that possess nuclear explosive devices should make available to other states nuclear explosive services for peaceful uses. Such a service would consist of performing the desired detonation under appropriate international observation, with the nuclear device remaining under the control and custody of the state that performs the service. This procedure would make available any possible future benefits of peaceful nuclear explosions at a cost far below that at which other countries could develop and produce such devices for themselves, especially in the case of excavation projects where only highly sophisticated thermonuclear explosives are really useful.

Paragraph 3 of Article 13 provides that appropriate officials shall have unrestricted access to any area in the vicinity of the explosion site. Since this could result in the compromise and divulging of sensitive design data of the nuclear device and of other techniques, we suggest that the officials only be given such access as is necessary to ensure compliance with paragraph 2 of this article.

Article 14

The United States understands that the Governments of Latin America represented on the Preparatory Commission are considering the question of the relationship of the agency to the Organization of American States (OAS). We concur that this question should be studied, and we believe that appropriate relationships with the OAS should be established. We suggest that Article 14 contain a provision stating

149

that appropriate relationships be concluded with the OAS. Our views on what these relationships could consist of are explained later.

Article 19

We suggest deletion of this article. Since paragraph 1 is subject to the consent of the parties, it adds nothing to Article 36 of the Statute of the International Court of Justice. Paragraph 2 fails to meet the requirements of paragraph 2 of Article 96 of the United Nations Charter.

Article 23

1. Regarding the question of the states that must ratify the proposed treaty prior to its entry into force, we note that the draft proposals contain two versions. In paragraph 1 of the left-hand column, it is implied that the treaty could enter into force when only two states had ratified, while paragraph 1 A of the right-hand column sets forth the requirement, based on Article 20, that all the states referred to in Article 20 must ratify the treaty before it can enter into force.

   As stated in the letter signed for the United States by William C. Foster and submitted to the Preparatory Commission on December 10, 1965, "The United States believes it important that all states in the area should participate. The refusal of certain states to participate would lead us to consider whether their exclusion might render the agreement ineffective or meaningless, or whether the agreement would still be worthwhile." The decision of whether the refusal of a certain state to participate in a Nuclear-Free Zone would render the agreement ineffective is in the first instance the decision of the states of the region. The United States hopes that the question of participation in a Latin American Nuclear-Free Zone will be duly resolved by the Governments of Latin America upon their thorough consideration of all existing conditions.

2. On the question of the relationship of the present nuclear powers to the proposed Nuclear-Free Zone, we also note that the draft proposals contain two versions. In Article 23, paragraph 1 B, the right-hand column calls for the signature and ratification by the nuclear powers of a protocol of guaranty prior to the entry into force of the treaty. Alternatively, Annex I of the draft proposals provides that the commitment of the nuclear powers to respect a Latin American Nuclear-Free Zone would be obtained by means of a United Nations General Assembly resolution after the treaty had been signed.

   Since the purpose of a Nuclear-Free Zone is to service as an aid in halting the proliferation of nuclear weapons, the United States believes that the first priority is for the states of the area concerned to agree on and enact the Nuclear-Free Zone. The United States does not believe that it is necessary to obtain guarantees of respect from nuclear powers prior to the entry into force of the zone. Our comments on appropriate means to obtain respect for the zone are contained in the following section.

Assurances of Respect for a Nuclear-Free Zone

Should an acceptable Latin American Nuclear-Free Zone Treaty be agreed upon, the United States would undoubtedly wish to join in a resolution under which, for example, the General Assembly welcomed the intention of those states approving the resolution to support and respect the treaty. However, the type of resolution contained in Annex I of the draft proposals assumes that binding, treaty-like commitments can be undertaken by voting for a General Assembly Resolution. Chapter IV of the United Nations Charter establishes that Assembly Resolutions are recommendatory. We could not accept an effort which would establish a contrary practice whereby, in supporting an Assembly Resolution, states would obligate themselves in the same way as if they had subscribed to a treaty. Furthermore, the use of a resolution such as that suggested in Annex I would also present us with difficult constitutional problems.

If the Preparatory Commission intends to seek a binding commitment from the nuclear powers to respect a Nuclear-Free Zone, we believe that the use of a protocol would be the most appropriate method. However, if a less formal and more generalized commitment would meet the needs of the contracting parties, the commission may wish to consider the use of a recommendatory General Assembly Resolution as mentioned above, or the request of individual declarations of intent from each of the nuclear powers to respect the Nuclear-Free Zone.

These comments do not, of course, represent a decision or obligation by the United States to undertake a commitment at this time. As we have previously indicated, our final position will have to await decisions by the Latin American states on that nature and scope of the proposed Nuclear-Free Zone.

Protocol of Guaranty II

We note that this protocol calls for the inclusion in the Nuclear-Free Zone by the states named of all those territories over which they exercise de jure or de facto responsibility. While the United States favors in principle the placing of appropriate territories in the Nuclear-Free Zone, we do not believe it is necessary to make this an all-inclusive policy. In some cases, existing political and international considerations could create difficulties in seeking to include territories. We believe that the states concerned should be invited to place territories in the Nuclear-Free Zone.

The United States has made clear in the December 10, 1965 letter its position regarding those areas over which it has responsibility. In that letter, we stated that "We do not wish to have included in the proposed Nuclear-Free Zone the Virgin Islands, since it is United States territory, or the Commonwealth of Puerto Rico, because of its integral relationship with the United States. In the case of both of these areas, the United States must deal with disarmament policies affecting other nuclear powers. From the United States point of view, we would be agreeable to inclusion of the Panama Canal Zone, although of course the well-established transit rights would not be affected by the establishment of the proposed Nuclear-Free Zone. We could also agree to include Guantanamo if Cuba participates."

International Atomic Energy Agency (IAEA) Relationship

As stated in previous occasions, the United States supports the utilization of the IAEA safeguards system in the proposed Nuclear-Free Zone. We strongly favor the initiative by the Latin American nations to submit their nuclear programs to IAEA safeguards. We would welcome an initiative to attach such safeguards on any nuclear material exported from the zone.

However, the IAEA cannot assume responsibility for control against the importation of nuclear weapons, since safeguards can only detect diversion from peaceful uses in specifically identified installations to which the IAEA has access. For verification against the introduction of nuclear weapons, other procedures must be considered, and we understand that this is the intent of Article 12, paragraph 1 B and C.

The United States hopes that the negotiation of the bilateral agreements between each contracting party and the IAEA will proceed promptly, but that unavoidable delays in their conclusion will not prejudice the establishment of an otherwise acceptable Nuclear-Free Zone, since other inspection procedures would be available under Article 12.

Relationship of the Agency to the OAS

The United States would like to suggest that the Preparatory Commission may wish to consider a cooperative arrangement between the Agency and the OAS patterned on specialized organization status. A precedent for such an arrangement is found in the cooperative arrangement authorized by the Council of the OAS on April 1, 1959 in the case of the United International Bureau for the Protection of Industrial, Literary, and Artistic Property. The report of the OAS Committee on that occasion (C-I-396, Rev. 3, April 1, 1959) contains valuable comments concerning the rationale for such arrangements.

The cooperative arrangement could include such things as periodic reports of the Agency's work; reports to the Council of the OAS on the annual budget and expenses; consultation on mutual problems; exchange of information, documents, and reports; and appropriate provisions for attendance at each other's meetings.

As indicated above, we suggest that Article 14 contain a provision stating that appropriate relationships be established with the OAS. In addition, we believe it would be desirable to amend paragraphs 6 and 8 of Article 12, along the lines suggested by the Venezuelan Delegation in document COPREDAL/L/14 dated May 1, 1966, to provide for submission of reports by the Secretary General of the Latin American Denuclearization Agency to the OAS. The United States also believes worthy of consideration the Venezuelan suggestion that paragraph 1 B of Article 12 be amended to provide that the assistance of the OAS and its specialized organizations be sought in certain cases.

Boundaries of Proposed Nuclear-Free Zone

The draft proposals do not clearly indicate the boundaries of the area within which the proposed Nuclear-Free Zone would be located. On the northern side, the 30th parallel, north latitude is mentioned in Articles 6, 20, and 23, but since this includes portions of the United States mainland, as well as Puerto Rico and the United States Virgin Islands, and excludes part of Mexico, we suggest that this be more precisely defined. On the southern side, we would recommend that the 60th parallel, south latitude be declared as the southern boundary, since that is the parallel referred to in the Antarctic Treaty as the northern limit of its application.

Sincerely yours,

(s.) Fulton Freeman
American Ambassador

Lic. Alfonso García Robles,
President of the Preparatory Commission for the Denuclearization of Latin America,
Secretariat of Foreign Relations, México, D. F.

22 Second Report of the Negotiating Committee of the Preparatory Commission for the Denuclearization of Latin America Concerning Informal Contacts with the Government of the People's Republic of China

1. The Preparatory Commission for the Denuclearization of Latin America, in its Resolution 12 (III) adopted unanimously on 3 May 1966, decided "to request the Negotiating Committee to make informal inquiries, in the manner and by the means it deems fit, to ascertain whether the Government of the People's Republic of China would be prepared to undertake to respect the legal instrument on the denuclearization of Latin America," and to request the Committee also "to transmit to the Governments of Member States a report on the results of its efforts before the opening of the Commission's fourth session."

2. As the result of a preliminary exchange of views between the three members of the Negotiating Committee at the time of the closing of the Third Session of the Commission, it was decided that when the Final Act of this period was reproduced, it should be translated not only into French, English, and Russian, as was done in the case of the previous final acts, but also into Chinese. Consequently, the Chairman of the Commission on 4 May addressed a note to the Secretary-General of the United Nations making the appropriate request, which was granted.

3. On the same occasion, the members of the Committee reached the conclusion that, before taking any action relative to the instructions that they had received from the Commission, they should wait for the document in which the Final Act would be reproduced in the Chinese language. They agreed, therefore, to reconsider this question as soon as this document was available.

4. When the members of the Committee were informed, in the middle of June, that the Chinese translation of document A/6328 was about to be completed, they met in New York City, headquarters of the United Nations, and on 17 and 18 June they carefully studied the various procedures that could be followed in order to carry out the instructions the Preparatory Commission had given to the Committee. As a result of the study, they reached the following conclusions:

(a) The method most likely to succeed in achieving the desired objective would certainly be for the members of the Committee to explain personally to the authorized representatives of the People's Republic of China the aims of the Treaty for the Denuclearization of Latin America, as well as the meaning and scope of the undertaking mentioned in operative paragraph 2 of Resolution 12 (III).

(b) For the purpose of doing all that is in their power to expedite the informal contacts referred to in the preceding paragraph, the members of the Committee should leave to the People's Republic of China the choice of an ambassador, accredited to any country with which the Member States of the Preparatory Commission maintain relations, through whom it may prefer to carry out such conversations, and they should demonstrate their willingness to move immediately to the country in which the ambassador thus chosen is resident.

(c) Inasmuch as none of the Governments of the Member States of the Preparatory Commission maintain diplomatic relations with the Government of the People's Republic of China, the Commission would have to communicate the foregoing through the good offices of some other government or by means of the personal services of an ambassador of one of the Member States of the Commission who, in the performance of his diplomatic functions, may have had the opportunity to establish personal relations with a high official of the Government of Peking and who, due to this, feels qualified to informally transmit to this Government the offer of the Negotiating Committee. Of these two alternatives, the members of the Committee believed that it would prefer the second, if it were feasible, because in that way the strictly and totally Latin American character of the undertaking of the Preparatory Commission would be shown.

5. After a rapid but intensive investigation, the members of the Committee learned that the Mexican Ambassador to the United Arab Republic, Eduardo Espinosa y Prieto, during the period from 1960 to 1965 when he was ambassador in Warsaw—a city in which, as is well known, the Ambassadors of the United States of America and of the People's Republic of China have had more than one hundred informal interviews—had had contact with Ambassador Wang Ping-nan, who at that time was dean of the diplomatic corps accredited to Poland and who today occupies the important post of First Deputy Minister of Foreign Affairs of his country. Ambassador Espinosa y Prieto was, therefore, immediately consulted and, after obtaining authorization from his Government, he agreed to make known to his former colleague, in an informal manner, the offer of the Negotiating Committee.

6. The communication in question took the form of a personal letter from Ambassador Espinosa y Prieto to First Deputy Minister Wang Ping-nan, dated in Cairo on 22 June and transmitted through the Ambassador of the People's Republic of China in Cairo, Huang Hua. In this letter, which included as annexes copies of the Final Act of the Third Session in Chinese, Spanish, and English, Ambassador Espinosa y Prieto stated the following:

> You can see in Resolution 12 (III) that a Negotiating Committee of the Latin American States has been requested to make contact with the representatives of the Pople's Republic of China to ascertain whether the latter would be prepared to undertake to respect the legal instrument on the denuclearization of Latin America.
>
> The Negotiating Committee has discussed this same question, in identical terms, with all the other nuclear powers of the world and now it has been instructed to do so with the Government of the People's Republic of China.
>
> In accordance with its terms of reference, the Negotiating Committee, which is composed of three Latin American plenipotentiaries, my compatriot Under-Secretary Alfonso García Robles, Ambassador José Sette Camara of Brazil, and Ambassador Leopoldo Benites Vinueza of Ecuador, wishes to establish contact with the representatives that the Government of the People's Republic of China may appoint for that purpose.
>
> The Committee is prepared to leave entirely to the discretion of the Government of the People's Republic of China the choice of its embassies and of its ambassadors through which the conversations in question should be carried out. . . . The members of the Committee are especially desirous of holding such conversations during the second half of June, if this should be possible.

156

7. On 8 August, the Ambassador of the People's Republic of China in Cairo, Huang Hua, made a personal visit to Ambassador Espinosa y Prieto, in order to make known to him verbally the reply of his Government to the offer of the Negotiating Committee. The main points of this reply can be as follows:

(a) The Government of the People's Republic of China, although it views with sympathy the efforts of the Latin American countries to denuclearize their zone, notes that all the activities in this connection are closely linked to a resolution of the General Assembly of the United Nations adopted in its Eighteenth Session.

(b) Inasmuch as the United Nations has violated all the rights of the People's Republic of China in the World Organization, China cannot participate in its activities and is therefore not in a position to support the Treaty for the Denuclearization of Latin America.

(c) The denuclearization of zones bordering on the United States of America will serve no purpose if the latter continues to maintain nuclear weapons in its territory and in its Latin American bases.

(d) The position of the People's Republic of China with regard to nuclear weapons has been announced several times and was expressed by its Government on the occasion of its first test of nuclear weapons made on 16 October 1964, in a declaration that stated:

The Chinese Government hereby solemnly declares that China will never at any time and under any circumstances be the first to use nuclear weapons. . . .

We sincerely hope that a nuclear war may never occur. We are convinced that, so long as all peace-loving countries and peoples of the world make common efforts and persist in the struggle, a nuclear war can be prevented.

The Chinese Government hereby formally proposes to the governments of the world that a summit conference of all the countries be convened to discuss the question of the complete prohibition and total destruction of nuclear weapons, and that as a first step, the summit conference should reach an agreement to the effect that the nuclear powers and those countries which may soon become nuclear powers undertake not to use nuclear weapons either against non-nuclear countries and nuclear-free zones, or against each other. . . .

We are convinced that nuclear weapons, which are after all created by man, certainly will be eliminated by man.

8. The Negotiating Committee deplores the failure of the above efforts to achieve the positive results desired by its members and,

on concluding its present report, wishes to render posthumous tribute to Ambassador Eduardo Espinosa y Prieto, who died a week ago on 22 August, for his invaluable and disinterested cooperation in the task that the Preparatory Commission entrusted to the Committee in its Resolution 12 (III).

Mexico City, 29 August 1966.

(SIGNED)

Ambassador Alfonso García Robles,
*Chairman of the Preparatory Commission
for the Denuclearization of Latin America*

(SIGNED)

Ambassador José Sette Camara,
Chairman of Working Group C.

(SIGNED)

Ambassador Leopoldo Benites,
Chairman of Working Group A.

23 Rules of Procedure of the Preparatory Commission for the Denuclearization of Latin America ▪ Approved at the Second Meeting of the Preparatory Commission ▪ held on 16 March 1965 ▪ and Revised at its Twenty-first Meeting ▪ held on 4 May 1966[9]

SESSIONS

Rule 1

The Preparatory Commission shall meet whenever a majority of its Members concurs in the request of any Member, or when the President convenes it.

Rule 2

The Secretary-General shall make available to the Members of the Commission, at least fifteen days before the opening of the regular session, complete sets of the documents prepared at the previous session and of the documents that any Member of the Commission may officially request from the Secretary-General.

Rule 3

The Secretary-General shall prepare the provisional agenda for each session and shall communicate it to the Members of the Commission,

[9] Unofficial translation.

whenever this is possible, no less than fifteen days before the opening of each session.

Rule 4

The provisional agenda of the session shall include such information and documents as the Secretariat may present concerning any question under consideration by it; the items proposed by any Member of the Commission; and those items which the Secretary-General deems appropriate for consideration by the Commission.

Rule 5

All items proposed for inclusion in the agenda shall be accompanied by an explanatory memorandum.

Rule 6

The provisional agenda of each session shall be submitted to the Commission for approval at the opening of the session.

DELEGATIONS

Rule 7

The delegation of a Member shall consist of one representative and of the alternate representatives and advisers designated by the nominating government.

Rule 8

An alternate representative or adviser may act as representative in the latter's absence.

Rule 9

The names of members of a delegation shall be submitted to the Secretary-General if possible not less than ten days before the date fixed for the opening of the session.

PRESIDENT AND VICE-PRESIDENTS

Rule 10

The Commission shall elect a President and two Vice-Presidents.

Rule 11

If the President finds it necessary to be absent during a meeting or any part thereof, he shall appoint one of the Vice-Presidents to his place.

Rule 12

A Vice-President acting as President shall have the same powers and duties as the President.

Rule 13

In addition to directing the discussions and exercising the powers which are conferred upon him elsewhere by these rules, the President shall rule on points of order, and, subject to these rules, shall take any measure related to the organization of the work of the Commission and shall respect the will of the majority of the Members of the Commission.

SUBSIDIARY ORGANS

Rule 14

The Co-ordinating Committee shall consist of the President of the Commission, who shall preside; the two Vice-Presidents or their representatives; and the Presidents of the working groups or their representatives. The Commission shall define the functions of the Committee. The Co-ordinating Committee shall not meet during the sessions of the Preparatory Commission unless the latter decides otherwise.

Rule 15

The Commission shall set up such working groups as it deems necessary for the performance of its functions. The reports of the working groups shall be referred to the Co-ordinating Committee before being submitted to the Commission.

Rule 16

The subsidiary organ shall adopt its own working procedure subject to the present rules of procedure.

Rule 17

A majority of the Members of a subsidiary organ shall constitute a quorum.

SECRETARIAT

Rule 18

The Secretary-General shall act in that capacity in all meetings of the Preparatory Commission, its Co-ordinating Committee and its other subsidiary organs. He may designate a member of the staff to act in his place at these meetings. The appointment of Secretariat staff to perform work outside the headquarters of the Commission shall require the consent of the Secretary-General.

Rule 19

The Secretariat shall be in charge of all administrative work of the Commission, including custody of the archives and publication of the documents. Furthermore, it shall perform all other work which the Commission may require.

LANGUAGES

Rule 20

Spanish, French, English and Portuguese shall be the official languages of the Preparatory Commission and its organs. Spanish shall be the working language.

RECORDS

Rule 21

Summary records of all plenary meetings of the Commission shall be drawn up and shall be circulated among the Members of the Commission.

Rule 22

All draft resolutions shall be submitted to the Secretariat in writing and may be presented in any of the official languages.

MEETINGS

Rule 23

The meetings of the Preparatory Commission shall be held in public unless the Commission itself decides that exceptional circumstances require that the meeting be held in private.

Rule 24

All decisions of the Commission taken at a private meeting shall be announced at the next public meeting.

Rule 25

A majority of the Members of the Preparatory Commission shall constitute a quorum.

Rule 26

The President shall call upon speakers in the order in which they signify their desire to speak. The President may call a speaker to order if his remarks are not relevant to the subject under discussion.

Rule 27

The Secretary-General, or his representative, may, at any time, make either oral or written statements to the Preparatory Commission concerning any question under consideration by it.

Rule 28

During the discussion of any matter, a representative may rise to a point of order, and the point of order shall be immediately decided by the President. If this decision is appealed, the President's ruling shall stand unless overruled by a majority of the Members.

Rule 29

During the discussion of the matter, a representative may move the adjournment of the debate. Before putting this motion to vote, only two representatives may speak in favor of, and two against, the motion.

Rule 30

A representative may at any time move the closure of the debate on the item under discussion. Permission to speak against closure of the debate shall be accorded only to two speakers, after which the motion shall be immediately put to the vote. The President may limit the time to be allowed to speakers under this rule.

Rule 31

Motions to suspend or adjourn the meeting shall be immediately put to the vote. The President may limit the time to be allowed to the representative making the motion.

Rule 32

Subject to Rule 28, the following motions shall have precedence in the following order over all other proposals or motions before the meeting: (*a*) to suspend the meeting; (*b*) to adjourn the meeting; (*c*) to adjourn the debate on the item under discussion; and (*d*) for the closure of the debate on the item under discussion.

Rule 33

Draft resolutions and amendments shall normally be introduced in writing and handed to the Secretary-General, who shall circulate copies to the delegations. As a general rule, no proposal shall be discussed or put to the vote unless copies of it have been distributed not later than the day preceding the meeting. The President may, however, recommend another procedure.

Rule 34

A motion may be withdrawn by its proposer at any time before voting on it has commenced, provided that the motion has not been amended. A motion which has thus been withdrawn may be reintroduced by any Member.

VOTING

Rule 35

Each Member of the Preparatory Commission shall have one vote.

Rule 36

The decisions of the Commission shall be made by a majority of the Members present and voting except when new items are introduced or when a question is deemed of sufficient importance by a majority to require the vote of two-thirds of the Members present and voting.

Rule 37

For the purposes of these rules, the phrase "Members present and voting" means Members casting an affirmative or negative vote. Members who abstain from voting are considered as not voting.

Rule 38

The Commission shall normally vote by show of hands or by standing, but any representative may request a roll-call. The roll-call shall be taken in the Spanish alphabetical order of the names of the Members, beginning with the Member whose name is drawn by lot. The name of each Member shall be called in any roll-call and its representative shall reply "yes," "no" or "abstention." The result of the voting shall be inserted in the record in the Spanish alphabetical order of the names of the Members.

Rule 39

After the President has announced the beginning of voting, no representative shall interrupt the voting except on a point of order in connection with the actual conduct of the voting.

Rule 40

Any representative may request that parts of a proposal or of an amendment be voted on separately.

Rule 41

When an amendment is moved to a proposal, the amendment shall be voted on first. When two or more amendments are moved to a proposal, the Commission shall first vote on the amendment furthest removed in substance from the original proposal and then on the amendment next furthest removed therefrom, and so on, until all the amendments have been put to the vote. Where, however, the adoption of one amendment necessarily implies the rejection of another amendment, the latter amendment shall not be put to the vote. If one or more amendments are adopted, the amended proposal shall then be voted upon. A motion is considered an amendment to a proposal if it merely adds to, deletes from, or revises part of the proposal.

Rule 42

If two or more proposals relate to the same question, the Commission shall, unless it decides otherwise, vote on the proposals in the order in which they have been submitted.

AMENDMENTS AND SUSPENSIONS OF THE RULES

OF PROCEDURE

Rule 43

These rules of procedure may be suspended by a majority of the Members of the Commission present and voting.

Rule 44

These rules of procedure may be amended by a two-thirds majority of the Members of the Commission.

24 Selected List of the Principal Documents of the Preliminary Meeting on the Denuclearization of Latin America and of the Preparatory Commission for Denuclearization of Latin America[10]

1. Summary records of the five meetings held by the Preparatory Commission. REUPRAL/AR/1 a 5, 23-27 November 1964.
2. Summary records of the eleventh to the twentieth meetings of the Coordinating Committee. COPREDAL/CC/AR/1 a 10, 7-14 March 1966.
3. Summary records of the first thirty-six meetings of the Preparatory Commission. COPREDAL/AR/1 a 36, 15 March 1965-30 August 1966.
4. Report of the Negotiating Committee. COPREDAL/CN/1, 20 December 1965.
5. Observations of the Mexican Government on the Preliminary Draft of the Multilateral Treaty for the Denuclearization of Latin America. COPREDAL/CC/OAT/1, 1 February 1966.
6. Complete text of the Preliminary Draft of the Multilateral Treaty for the Denuclearization of Latin America, in accordance with the observations of the Mexican Government. COPREDAL/CC/OAT/1 Anexo, 1 February 1966.

[10] The documents in this list exist only in Spanish. Excluded are those reproduced in this appendix.

7. Corrigendum to the observations of the Mexican Government, to which the above number refers, and to the annex of this document. COPREDAL/CC/OAT/1 Corr., 1 February 1966.

8. Observations of the Chilean Government on Resolution 9 (II). COPREDAL/CC/OAT/2, 1 February 1966.

9. Working Paper submitted by the Coordinating Committee to the Preparatory Commission for preparation of the Preliminary Draft of the Treaty for the Denuclearization of Latin America. COPRE-DAL/CC/DT/1, 14 March 1966.

10. Draft of the Treaty for the Denuclearization of Latin America, presented by the Delegations of Brazil and Colombia. COPREDAL/L/13, 26 April 1966.

11. Note addressed to the President of the Preparatory Commission by the Cuban Ambassador to Mexico, headquarters of the Commission, concerning the attitude of his Government. COPREDAL/46, 21 July 1966.

12. Note addressed to the President of the Preparatory Commission by the Nicaraguan Ambassador to Mexico, headquarters of the Commission, concerning the note reproduced in the document COPRE-DAL/46. COPREDAL/48, 2 August 1966.

13. Note addressed to the President of the Preparatory Commission by the Netherlands Ambassador to Mexico, headquarters of the Commission, concerning the attitude of his Government. COPREDAL/49, 11 August 1966.

14. Note of the Uruguayan Chargé d'Affaires transmitting the observations of his Government on Resolution 14 (III). COPREDAL/OAT/2, 18 July 1966.

15. Note addressed to the Secretary-General of the Commission by the Chilean Minister of Foreign Affairs transmitting the observations of his Government on Resolution 14 (III). COPREDAL/OAT/3, 9 August 1966.

16. Note addressed to the Secretary-General of the Commission by the Venezuelan Chargé d'Affaires transmitting the observations of his Government on Resolution 14 (III). COPREDAL/OAT/4, 13 August 1966.

17. List of the documents issued by the Preliminary Meeting on the Denuclearization of Latin America and by the Preparatory Commission for Denuclearization of Latin America between 21 November 1964 and 25 August 1966. COPREDAL/S/25, 25 August 1966.